No Money Startup: How To Build An Apparel
Manufacturing Company
Copyright 2014 by Sumiyyah A. Rasheed

Printed in the United States of America

First Printing: 2014

I0483115

Dedication

This book is dedicated to my mom and dad, Viola and Samuel Williams, who believed in my vision and supported me in the darkest times, believing I would be successful in my endeavor. Thanks so very much for your help and encouragement.

Acknowledgements

I would like to acknowledge Pat Lonon, owner of Cover It Up, as a mentor and confidante over the past 20 years brainstorming and plotting strategy every Sunday morning. Francine Sly and her sister Michelle Saffel who worked tirelessly over the years to help me bring my vision to life and Jamal Glen for his exceptional photography.

A big thank you to my mom Viola Williams (Wala Rasheed), sons Javier and Hussamiddin, my daughter Shareefah who worked long hours developing patterns, fitting models, sewing samples, spreading and cutting fabric along with other duties as required. Thanks to the grandchildren who ate lots of pizza at my lick'em and stick'em letter and promotional mailing parties.

I couldn't have come this far in the fashion and apparel manufacturing industry without the expertise of Sylvia Payton, designer, sample and pattern maker extraordinaire who worked over and beyond the call of duty and Ms. Estella McGinity first rate sewing operator and instructor.

A special acknowledgement to LaShanda Henry, on-line marketing guru, Charles Major The Mogul, Richelle Shaw The Million Dollar Equation marketing guru, and, of course, Ann McIndoo, my Author's Coach, who got this book out of my head.

Contents

Introduction

As I worked on my business, people have asked me repeatedly can you write down how you started. What are the steps? What's the secret? So finally I put pen to paper to explain, give guidance and hope to those who are smitten with the idea of being a fashion entrepreneur but don't believe they have the funds to go for it. What I want you, the reader, to walk away with are the basic tools to start and maintain an apparel manufacturing company to produce your line.

In 2003 when I first thought about my apparel manufacturing company startup I was already self-employed as an Information Technology (IT) consultant. The reason for the second startup was to build another income stream, provide jobs for my family members and make a positive impact on society through charity. Initially, I tried making clothes in China, India, and Pakistan but the long lag times and sometimes poorly constructed garments caused deep moments of frustration and missed ship dates. Because I didn't have a background in apparel manufacturing, I needed to become knowledgeable about production planning, supply chain management, pattern development and factory setup. So how did I learn the manufacturing process? I got off my duff and traveled the world observing and analyzing manufacturing procedures in Mexico, China, Pakistan, India, Turkey and Morocco. I backpacked, took notes and analyzed the processes.

When I returned home from each trip I added something new to my blossoming business process.

To start a business takes nerves of steel and a specific mindset. There's a difference between being an entrepreneur and a jobseeker. A jobseeker merely wants a paycheck to pay the bills and somewhere to park his/her feet every day for 8 hours. On the other hand an entrepreneur possesses a deep passionate love for his or her product and will work relentlessly to bring life to the dream. I started my business in the worst economic recession and thrived during the housing crash, the Wall Street crash, and the bank industry debacle. Why? How? Because I have a timeless skill set. With over 800,000 jobs lost over the past decades to off shoring, desired manufacturing skillsets among Americans has been lost. In addition, Americans have lost the edge in ingenuity moaning and groaning about how they don't know what to do if I lose my job. At the time of my startup my goal was to make a job for myself without waiting for a handout from the government. My goal was and is to leave a legacy for my grandchildren to step into without worrying about shoveling resumes in front of incompetent managers and struggling to find a job.

What I impart in my book are tried and true methods to starting and maintaining an apparel manufacturing company. Young people are caught in a cycle of instant gratification from cell phones, IPad, notebooks and sophisticated games, and many hours per week of reality shows, so they unwittingly believe anything they want to accomplish should happen at least in 30 minutes or overnight. **NOT!** So rather than join the course of naysayers, I decided to take matters into my own hands and blaze a trail into the unknown.

I grew tired of hearing you can't compete with China, they're too big and they can produce items cheaply. You'll never do it. Well, I may not be able to compete with the Chinese, Indians, Vietnamese, or other low wage countries on price but I can beat them hands down on quality and speed to market.

So what do I want you to take away from this book? I want you to be inspired to take action. Move on your dream and know that it is possible to have a manufacturing facility no matter the size and do for yourself without relying on handouts. So what is apparel manufacturing? I asked myself that question when I first started and I'm sure you're asking yourself that question now. It's taking your idea and turning it into a tangible dress, suit, lingerie or pants. But how do you do that? What's the process? What are the components? How do I get there?

These are all valid questions which I answer in the following chapters. Don't worry if you don't know how to sew or make a pattern, we'll go through all those steps. You'll learn about pattern and sample making, spreading/cutting, and the world of sourcing fabric. Where do I get my fabric? Is it in the backyard? No! It could be in New York. It can take you to Paris. It can take you to Shanghai. You'll learn how to source fabric.

You'll also become well versed in production planning, supply chain management, and logistics. These are points that aren't necessarily covered in fashion design school, but are points you need to know if you're going to enter the wonderful world of apparel manufacturing.

The benefits of being your own manufacturer is control of the whole process from start to finish. This means you're able to take your idea and walk it through all the steps to final product without layers of approval and long lead times.

The startup and maintenance steps we'll cover are from my perspective down in the trenches -- planning and production. I wasn't formally educated in fashion merchandising and factory operations, but believe me, by working in the trenches and getting my hands dirty, I've received an excellent education from the School of Hard Knocks in apparel manufacturing. I want to share with you the ups and downs and hopefully help you avoid some of the pitfalls of being a manufacturer.

Chapter One

Acting on the idea is the first step and one of the key components to a successful business launch. A solid business plan, persistence, capital integrated with a can-do spirit will help you reach your goal. ---Sumiyyah A. Rasheed

The notion of starting an apparel manufacturing business may be a daunting task to individuals who have financial constraints. Marketing, financial and business plans, and the whole idea of startup can over whelm you to the point of emotional paralysis. To avoid emotional paralysis, careful planning and analysis is the answer. The simplest way to conquer the seemingly insurmountable task of startup is to break the startup task into small bite size components that are achievable.

Determine what type of manufacturer you will be

Right after you determine your legal structure, whether it is a sole proprietor, LLC, incorporation, you will have to determine if you will manufacture for designers and retailers as an independent contractor or if you will manufacture your own collection. Either way you will have to hire staff such as cutters, sewing operators, designers, pattern makers, and sample makers.

In this book I cover how I started my apparel manufacturing company from the ground up to produce my own collection and sell directly to retailers. When there were slow periods, I manufactured small production runs for local designers, but the majority of my company's work was and is producing my own collection.

The small manufacturing company has a few unique challenges not faced by other small businesses. First, you need adequate financial resources to contend with rapid changes in the fashion trends and styles, second, the decrease of peripheral suppliers, and availability of skilled labor, third, the growing competition from other small apparel manufacturers which are tightening the market.

As you think through and develop your business plan, keep in mind how you will handle these key challenges. Think about how your business will be operated. For example, how will you process new orders? What processes and tools will you use for customer services? As you think through these processes document them as they will become the basis of your company's standard operating procedure (SOP). A standard operating procedure is a step-by-step instruction guide explaining how a task in your organization should be performed.

I have an SOP for the cutting room, the administrative office, and the sewing room. I can't impress upon you enough how critical your company's SOP is to your operation. Let me give you an example, of what happens when you don't have an SOP.

Company XYZ has been in business for 2 years and Sally is the administrative assistant. Every morning she opens and sorts the mail, enters employee hours into a spreadsheet, and purchases equipment for the company.

Sally and two of her friends go to the mountains for a weekend of skiing and fun. However, Sally had so much fun she twisted her ankle and won't be able to work for two weeks. So who will perform the office tasks during her absence? Basically any temporary worker can come in and sort the mail and enter worker hours in a spreadsheet. What the temporary worker can't do is call the customs office and check on inbound shipments and arrange for delivery. This is a small but important task Sally performs but has never documented. Without the calls to the customs broker and the proper paperwork completed, all inbound orders will sit in the warehouse with fees accumulating every day. With the inbound product sitting in a warehouse, company XYZ is losing money simply because one person has all the knowledge in her head and the process was never documented.

You may take the office, warehouse or production tasks for granted, assuming anyone can step in and perform the task when key personnel are not available. A word of caution is to be prepared and **WRITE IT DOWN!**

Determine the Business Structure

Let's talk about the types of business structures available to choose from. You have an idea, so now what? How do you turn this idea into reality? One of the first steps is to determine your business structure or legal entity for your business. There are three types.

- LLC
- Sole Proprietor
- S Corporation

Limited Liability Corporation or LLC

The Limited Liability Corporation or LLC, shields the business from personal lawsuits, offers full-time limited liability protection to all owners like the corporation, and yet has a pass through tax status like a partnership. It's regulated by the state in which you're doing business. Do a bit of research to determine if you're complying with the laws of the state you're transacting your business in. You can also go the IRS website at www.IRS.gov/business/small to read more.

Sole Proprietorship

The Sole Proprietorship is owned and operated by an individual with no distinction between the business and the individual; any business debts are the individual's personal responsibility. One of the main disadvantages of a sole proprietorship is unlimited liability where the owner's personal assets can be taken away in the event of a lawsuit. When I initially started my business I chose the sole proprietorship because it was the easiest way to get up and running. However, in later years I decided to go to an incorporated status.

S Corporation

The "S" Corporation In general does not pay any Federal income taxes, but instead the corporation's income or losses are divided and passed through to its shareholders. The shareholders must then report the income or loss on their own individual income tax returns.

Accounting

Accounting is a huge part of your business because you need a system to help track your expenses and sales; as well as generate profit and loss statements in order to give you a view of where money is being spent. Moreover, an accounting system will give you a complete and accurate picture of your financial status. Why is this important? For example, let's say you want to apply for a small business loan or credit with a supplier. The first thing they'll say is, "I'll need your financial documents, meaning a profit and loss statement so they can properly assess your credit worthiness. Even if you are not thinking of applying for credit or a loan, tending to your accounting responsibilities will:

Give you a clear picture of your spending habits, give you a clear picture of areas where waste can controlled and help with organization and discipline.

You don't have to be a tech geek to use accounting software. Just a little time and reading will help you get up and running.   Listed below is a partial list of accounting software tools you can choose from.

- o FreshBooks
- o QuickBooks

Business License

What is a business license? The business license is a document issued by the county or city depending on where you live and allows you to operate a business in the specified area. You can use your license to purchase items at a wholesale versus a retail level. Buying at a wholesale level is a huge cost savings over straight retail. Contact your local government, county or city, to determine where to obtain your business license.

Business Checking Account

I am going to put this in bold letters **KEEP YOUR PERSONAL and BUSINESS ACCOUNT SEPARATE!** Why? Expenses for the business should be paid for by the business. Personal and home expenses should be paid for by personal money. Keep your personal money separate from your business money so you won't overspend or get it mixed up. For example, the rent for your business should be paid from your business account. Not your personal checking account. Following this practice will be a nightmare when it comes time to reconcile your taxes and expenses. Take your business license to your bank and open a business checking account under "Doing Business As" or DBA. Be sure to ask what perks are available for business accounts such as free checking, lines of credit or discounts.

Employee Identification Number (EIN)

Employee Identification Number or EIN is obtained from the IRS and is also known as your Federal Tax Identification Number which is used to identify your business entity. You can go to www.IRS.gov/business to get more information.

Attorney and Accountant

As you set up your business there are two critical team members you need. The first is an attorney and if you can find one that is familiar with the apparel business that's even better. The second is an accountant to help you file your taxes and give you advice regarding your 401k and other investments and expenditures. To save money I track my expenses and income in an accounting software tool. At year end I total my expenses in my spreadsheet with a column for the name of the expense and a second column for the item amount. I give the soft or electronic copy to my accountant. Boy does he love me because everything is neatly organized and it makes his life so much easier while preparing my taxes.

Business Insurance

Be sure you have proper insurance for your business. If you're working from home, upgrade your current homeowners insurance to encompass your business equipment, files, computer, and anything you're using to conduct business. If your plan is to rent office space, you will usually need a minimum of one million dollars commercial liability insurance. You can call your insurance agent and explain you're opening a business and ask for their suggestions and advice. If your agency is not able to write the policy, ask for a referral to someone who can write the policy.

Financing Your Startup

There are several ways new business owners can finance a startup, which include an SBA Loan, Bank Loan, Investors, personal savings and credit cards. Whatever you do when you initially start up

DON'T QUIT YOUR DAY JOB!

You'll need every last penny you can salvage to fund your business expenses, unexpected emergencies and personal expenses. Hold onto your day job until you have enough income from your entrepreneurial adventure to match or exceed your 9-5 check. Let's take a look at the first option for financing a startup.

Small Business Administration or SBA: Before you show up at the Small Business Administration office you'll need a business plan in hand and collateral.

Since I didn't use a loan to startup, I am not going to elaborate on the process. However, you can go to www.SBA.gov and look at the information and criteria for obtaining an SBA loan.

Other options include: Bank Loans, Venture Capitalists, Investors, Family/Friends, Savings and/or Credit Cards. If none of this works or you're rejected, I would suggest taking the route I pursued —get a second job. I recommend a second job rather than working overtime on your present job, because the overtime will be heavily taxed and you'll only receive a few measly dollars. So it's better to get a second job to finance your business startup and use it solely for your business.

Another alternative is to save money from your current check to help finance your startup. Think of the savings as an investment in you. With these funds open your business account, so you will have money set aside to use for all startup expenses. Think as if you are investing in another company's stock, but this is stock in you. I used my second job's income to pay for things such as advertising costs, business cards, license fees, office equipment and a new phone line. All of this was important for me to get started so I earmarked that money especially for startup.

Venture Capital

Angel investors --- Here are some sources you can explore: Pi Capital, The Go Big Network and The Angel Investor Network, which help to bring angels and entrepreneurs together. Check out Guy Kawasaki blog, "How to Change the World." It has great information on how to raise capital using the Angel's method.

Accounting

Decide whether to use the cash or accrual system of accounting. Choose the fiscal year, which is usually January through December and setup a record keeping system for all payments to and from your business.

Consider hiring a bookkeeper or accountant to help you with system configuration. Start with a file folder for each month for your receipts and at the end of that month tape them to paper. I know this sounds rudimentary but it works when you're first getting started. Tape your receipts to paper, itemize the category or title, staple them together & put them back in the folder. I would turn that over to the bookkeeper and go through the entries and make sure all your expenses are accounted for.

At the end of the year, as you get ready to file your taxes, everything is nice, neat and organized. You have your hard copy and create a soft copy in a spreadsheet that you can give it to the accountant to easily file your taxes.

Business Plan

You'll want to write a business plan, including your profit and loss forecasts and cash flow analysis. You can start with a one page plan or do a full-blown business plan. The point is to write something. A business plan is a living document, a roadmap for your business, an evolving process that can and should be tweaked along the way. If you aren't sure how to start or you feel intimidated by writing a business plan, you can call your local university or

Chamber of Commerce and ask if they have a business incubator and enroll yourself. You will get specialized help from tutors who will coach you through all the research and writing steps.

As part of the business plan coaching, you will conduct the research and each week as you finish a section the coach will check your plan and make suggestions. When you contact the incubator, tell them you need help right away and be emphatic because you'll need this plan to guide you through your business startup.

I used the University of Georgia's Business Incubator which was housed in my local Chamber of Commerce. I had a wonderful coach who really helped me understand business planning. It was grueling but I did the work and it was worth it.

Simple business plan outline

1. Executive Summary
2. Company Description
3. Product or Service
4. Market Analysis
5. Strategy and Implementation
6. Management Team
7. Financial Analysis

Patents

Any logos or proprietary property should be patented. You can go to www.uspto.gov/ to get information about how to do the research and find out how to patent your logo or any other proprietary information.

What Is Proprietary Information?

This can be anything you've developed. Let's say you've developed a specialized pattern technique and you want it patented. Call the office or go to the website to start the process and research how to patent your item. This is critical because, unfortunately, oftentimes ideas are stolen. We all have ideas, but if it's something specialized to your business, then it's important to have it patented.

Setting Goals and Staying Committed

I'm often asked, "How do I get started"? For those of you who are newbies, I would like to share one of my comments on Startup Nation's website (www.startupnation.com).

> *Acting on the idea is the first step and one of the key components to a successful business launch. A solid business plan, persistence, and the can-do spirit will help you reach your goal. Building your business is a life-long*

commitment and if you're not in it for the long haul, then don't start down the road.

I'd also add keep the negative folks away from you. They are dream killers.

---Sumiyyah Rasheed

Goal Setting

What does your business look like in 2, 4 or 5 years? Will it be a small home based business or is it a large corporation with employees?   Whatever your vision is, you'll need a road map and goals to help you achieve your vision.

To achieve your vision it is important to set realistic goals. Start out by categorizing your goals in to three categories.   Those categories are short, mid and long term goals.   Short term goals are milestones you want to complete say from the present to 1 year. These may be goals such as to secure an office building, sell 50 units of your product or build your customer base. Mid-term goals have a time line of 1 – 3 years. During the this period you can improve your company's infrastructure by adding dedicated customer services personnel, a sales rep or any number of goals you want to set for yourself. The long term goals have a time line of 5 years and up. Take time to imagine what your life would look like. What is the vision of your business? The sky is the limit! But keep in mind to have a mechanism in place to hold yourself accountable.

To begin with, as I stated earlier, set **REALISTIC** time lines and goals. I put the word realistic in caps and bold font to draw your attention to the word. What happens to many entrepreneurs in the early years is they set huge goals with short timeframes. Going down this road will cause you to become overwhelmed and paralyzed to the point where you won't take any action because there are too many tasks to be completed and very little planning and time. Always break your goals down into small components and be specific. What do you really want to accomplish? Just saying I want to make more money or I want to start my own business isn't a solid goal.   Why? Because, there isn't a time line or specific amount of money that defines the objective. If you pursue the goal "I want more money" you'll never achieve the goal. The reason - You don't know how much you want. You want something but nothing specific. What does your business look like in 2, 4 or 5 years? What are the steps to achieve your vision?

To make things simple for you, complete the "Goal Setting Exercise" I've laid out here.

Goal Setting Exercise – Part One

Answer these questions---

Where do you see yourself in 5 years?

How much time are you willing to put into the business?

Is this a hobby or something you are willing to put energy into?

Take a blank sheet of paper and write at the top of it Business Goals.

Just start writing all of the business goals that come to mind. Don't try to categorize them just write and keep writing until you've exhausted your list of goals.

Now, take three (3) sheets of paper for the second portion of the exercise.

Sheet 1 – label this one "Short Term Goals"

Review your general list of business goals and from that list choose those goals that you feel are short term goals. Nothing is concrete so don't feel the item has to stay on this list. It can change and please don't be afraid of change.

Sheet 2 – label this one "Mid Term Goals"

Review your general list of business goals and from that list choose those goals that you feel are mid-term goals.

Sheet 3 – label this one "Long Term Goals"

Review your general list of business goals and from that list choose those goals that you feel are long term goals.

Goal Setting Exercise – Part Two

Now take the sheet marked "Short Term Goals" and go down the list and arrange the items according to a time frame. Ask yourself what needs to be accomplished first, second, and so on. See the sample list below to help you get started.

Item	Date
Business license	
Business cards	
Purchase office equipment	
Business fliers	
Networking events	
Website development	

Identifying and setting up your business entity, writing your business plan, building your financial and legal team, as well as goal setting are critical components to build and maintain a successful company.

Chapter 1 Summary:

Before you do anything related to your business, think about the outcome. Where do you see yourself in 2, 5, 10 years. Ask yourself if you can work for months without receiving a steady paycheck. Do you need stability to feel a sense of comfort? Can you work on a task without giving up when faced with a challenge? If you can honestly answer that you can accomplish these tasks, then you're probably cut out to be a fashion entrepreneur.

Checklist:

Consult with an Accountant

Write a Business Plan

Obtain Business Insurance

Decide where to house your business (optional if you are not planning to work from home)

Determine your startup costs

Decide on a Company Logo

Obtain Business Cards

List of start-up tasks

Determine your startup costs

Ddecide on a Company Logo

Build a Website

Chapter Two

Where Do I Start?

A life spent making mistakes is not only more honorable, but more useful than a life spent doing nothing. --- George Bernard Shaw

In the previous chapter I discussed general business ideas, but now I'll turn my attention to the specific reason for this book, launching a small manufacturing business from the ground up. The question you are probably asking now is, "Where do I start"? Really the best place to start is at home. In the minds of some individuals a business isn't a business unless you are in a professional office setting. To save money and grow your business you have to start small. However, starting small doesn't mean you think small. On the contrary, keep the big ideas and constantly nurture them, but the physical business operation is better off in a small space until you outgrow it. Think of some the well-known business that started out small. My favorite, Ben and Jerry's, started with savings of $8,000.00 in an old barn, the late Steve Jobs started Apple in his garage, and Michele Hoskins of **Michele Foods, Inc.** started her syrup company in her mother's basement, while

Chief Shoe Giver, Blake Mycoskie of TOMS Shoes began his business in a shared apartment.

So for you the fashion entrepreneur, the barn, the garage, the basement, the bedroom, or the apartment are ideal choices.

I started my manufacturing company using my living and family rooms as the sewing operation and converting my garage into the cutting, quality control and shipping area. Back then, my sewing operation consisted on three machines; a commercial straight stitch, a three thread serger and a double needle machine.

Starting a cut and sew operation isn't difficult, however, maintaining the operation has its challenges. The main components of a cut and sew operation are sewing and cutting room equipment. Before purchasing any equipment determine where you will house your business. Will you rent space or work from home? I strongly suggest save money and work from home as the best option. There are pros and cons to working from home, but with discipline and organization, the work at home option can be beneficial. The obvious pro to a home-based startup is low overhead while the obvious con is lack of a defined home/business environment.

A home based cut and sew operation requires industrial machinery versus home sewing machines and sergers. What's the best type of sewing equipment? Where will I purchase commercial sewing equipment? How do I know which type of sewing equipment is right for me and my business? To help you answer these questions use the chart below to narrow your answers.

Equipment – Where to purchase

The sewing equipment needed in your sewing

Fabric Category	Equipment	Model
Woven	Straight stitch, 5 thread serger, blind hemmer	Juki, Brother, Singer
Non-woven	Straight stitch, 5 thread serger or 3 thread serger, overlock, blind hemmer(optional)	Juki, Brother, Singer
Lingerie and intimate apparel	Straight stitch, 5 thread serger or 3 thread serger, overlock	Juki, Brother, Singer

room isn't your regular home sewing machine as you'll need a commercial straight stitch machine and its function is solely to sew a straight line without fancy or decorative stitches. The difference between home machines and commercial machines is size, power and function. While home machines are slower and multifunctional, commercial machines, however, have specific functions and are much faster.

To find commercial equipment, start with the local sewing machine outlet. They may not have the machine you desire but they should be able to direct you to companies that have commercial equipment.

When you call your local machine person, be specific and tell them you want a machine that has a table and a motor so they will understand you are talking about an industrial machine. If you'll be working from home, ask them to convert the motor so it will run on house current. The majority of industrial machines are purchased from companies that have gone out of business and they run on a different electrical current.

It doesn't cost much, maybe $100, to have the motor converted. Even if you're going to rent a space, it's important to have the motor converted in order to avoid overloading the facilities circuits.

Serger

The serger is used during garment construction to finish seams. A serger has a looping function that locks the thread over the material. Serger models you can use in your operation are Juki, Singer or Brother. There are two types of commercial serger. They are the three and the five thread machines. The difference between the two is the five thread serger has a safety lock stitch while the three thread only has the loopers.

The three thread serger is normally used for knitwear while the five thread is used for woven and non-woven fabric, because the five thread serger has the straight stitch, which expedites the garment production process. It will expedite the work because along with serging the machine will sew a straight stitch for seam reinforcement as one process. Whereas the three thread serger will only perform the overlocking function. My suggestion is to purchase a five thread. To view models of the serger see figures 1 and 2 on the following page.

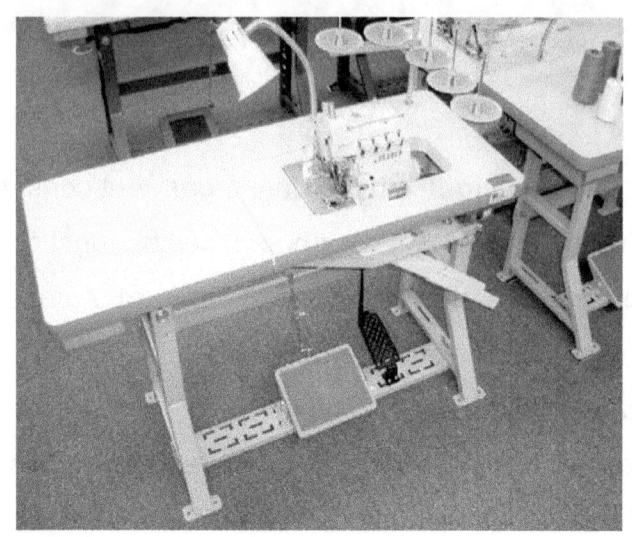

Figure - 1 Juki 5 thread serger

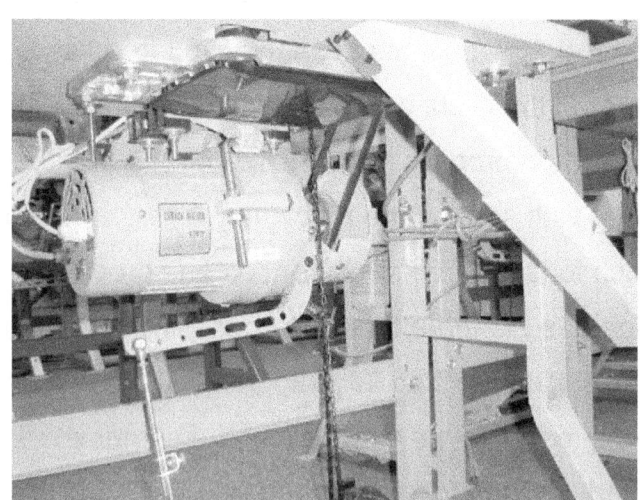

Figure - 2 Juki Serger Motor

Cutting Tables

Even if you begin working from home, you'll want to start with commercial tables because of sturdiness and durability. If you have the space, you can get the industrial tables which come in four-foot sections. If you don't have the room, you can get tables from your local fabric store or make your own. Prior to purchasing my commercial table, I made my cutting table from doors purchased from a local home improvement store and applied legs to get the desired height. Shown below is a photo of an 8 section commercial table. The full length is 32ft. or 4ft x 8 sections.

Figure - 3 Commercial cutting with 8 parts

Sewing Room Equipment

In your sewing room you will need: Fairgate rulers, hip curves, French curves, tape measures, scissors, marking pencils, fabric weights, pattern hole punch, pattern notcher, cutting knife, and thread. You can get these pieces from South Star Supply in Nashville, Tennessee. They are my favorite go-to source for all the components you'll need to startup. In the following sections are images of some of the tools you'll need and brief descriptions.

Fairgate Rulers: You'll need 12, 18 and 36 inch rulers for various tasks. I suggest purchasing clear and steel rulers for your tool set.

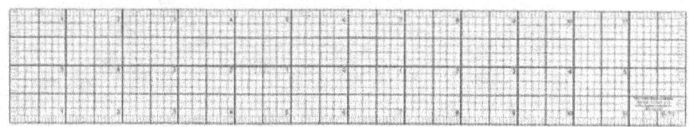

Figure 4 - Clear 18 inch ruler

Hip Curve: This is the instrument used when developing a pattern to draw the hip curve.

French Curve: This is used for drawing the arm and neck area of a pattern, which is an important piece.

The hip and French curve can be purchased at your local fabric store or you can order them online.

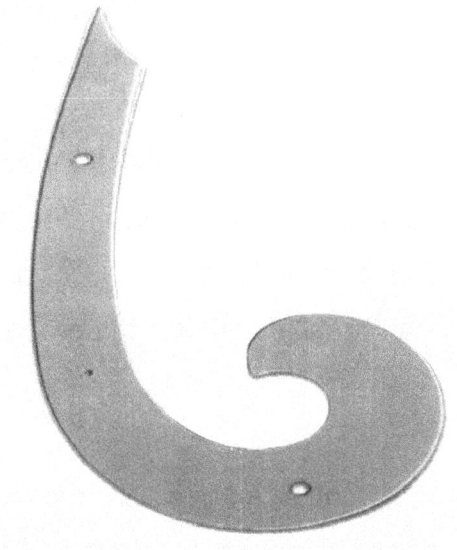

Figure - 5 French Curve

Tape Measure: It can be purchased from a local store in 60 or 120 inch lengths.

Scissors: I prefer Gingher (there are other brands) because they're sturdier and a better quality steel. My suggestion is to purchase at least two pair a 6" and maybe 10" scissors.

Needles: The commercial sewing machines require specific needles and if not inserted properly, meaning the groove on the shaft of the needle is not facing the proper direction, the machine won't operate properly. Before purchasing your needles determine the make and model of your machine. Once you determine the sewing manufacturer and type of fabric you'll use, ask the salesperson what size needle is the best to use. For example, if you're sewing a lot of silk you'll need a thinner needle. However, If you're working with denim you'll need a heavier needle, but be sure the salesperson understands what you're sewing so they can provide you with the proper needles.

Bobbins: Machine bobbins will come with the machine, but be sure to buy extra bobbins. When you're running production and churning through a lot of fabric, you'll find threads will break and bobbins can break or bend. Best option, keep at least 10-20 bobbins on-hand for specific machines.

Fabric Weights: The fabric weights are used to hold fabric in place while spreading and cutting. There's a weight that's about six inches long and looks like a flat iron with a handle or you can use clamps. Pictured below is what I call the flat iron version.

Figure 6 Fabric Weight

Pattern Punch: This looks like a rabbit ear and we sometimes call them that. A Pattern Punch is used to punch holes in patterns so you can hang them for storage.

Figure 7 - Pattern Hole Punch

Shelves: To store your books, fabric and supplies, shelving purchased from your local home improvement store will serve well.

Office Equipment

Desk: Not too large, that fits comfortably in a corner, with good storage space.

File Cabinet: Preferably one that's fireproof, because you don't want to lose your important documents.

File Folders: Depending on the size of your cabinet you can get two types, either legal size or letter size.

Computer: A desktop is okay but a laptop is preferred so you can carry it with you if need be. On the computer you should have an anti-virus program and include an external hard drive as well for periodic backups of your data. Trust me on this, I've had my laptop crash at least twice and have lost tons of pattern making and business information that couldn't be recovered. For a minimal fee of around $139 you can get an external hard drive, but there's no point in having the hard drive if you don't use it, which means you need to have a weekly backup of everything on your system. Get in the habit, make it a weekly practice.

A good computer backup practice to use is Friday afternoons before closing down backup your laptop. This way in case it crashes, you've only lost a week versus years of information. This is a critical yet beneficial point.

Printer: There are tons of printers to choose from and they are relatively inexpensive. The best office solution is a multifunctional printer that can scan, copy, and print. You'll lose time if you have to race to your local copy center in order to copy, print or scan documents. In your operations you want efficiency and flexibility to save time.

Storage Bins: These will be used in your cutting room area and should be clear so you can see the contents. The bins can be used to house fabrics, accessories, trim or even files.

Separate Phone Line or Cell Number: You don't want to use your personal cell as your business line, as those lines should be separate. For incoming business calls you want to answer professionally each time you receive a call. If your business is Sally's ABC manufacturing, that's how you should answer, "Good morning, Sally's ABC Manufacturing Company, may I help you?"

If you don't use your business line and use a personal cell phone, you may miss a call or may answer inappropriately, which can cause you to lose business. You will be known by your tone and the way you answer your phone. To impress the caller, your voice should be chipper and always come across as professional.

Square Card Reader: You can get this nifty item on-line at www.**square**up.com/ or through PayPal (www.paypal.com). Customers generally don't carry cash these days. So as not to lose out on a sale you need wireless capability. The square card reader is so cool because you can accept payment literally anywhere. For instance, if you're out and about at a tradeshow, you can take it with you. Or if customers call in, you have the ability to take care of a transaction via credit card over the phone.

Cutters

Producing small or large runs, commercial cutters instead of scissors are the tools of choice. Depending on the job size, there are specific size and style commercial cutters you can use.

When I first started I didn't know a thing about spreading and cutting, so I cut by hand and that's not good. Save your hand and invest in a small electrical rotary cutter. The one I used for years is called Little Delilah and cost $125.   It can be purchased from South Star Supply and was the best investment I ever made. It can cut approximately two inch ply – a ply being the number of fabric layers.

As your business grows you'll have to invest in a cutting knife, which is different than a rotary cutter. A cutting knife is a straight blade that vibrates up and down at a very fast pace in order to cut the fabric. As my business grew, I purchased a 6 inch Eastman cutting knife and at this point I was cutting 25 to 50 ply and needed the power. Depending on your needs and whether you're cutting denim, cotton or silk, you'll need a specific cutter for each particular job. Currently I have three cutters, the small rotary cutter, a mid-sized rotary cutter and I have my big knife for bigger jobs. If I'm cutting denim, up to 10 layers, I'm not going to use my rotary cutter. It's up to you to decide, at the point when you accept a job or if you're running your production, what type of cutter you're going to use.

Eastman Straight Knives

The Eastman line of straight knife machines have set the industry standard for quality, performance, and engineering for over 120 years. Here a couple of photos of my knives.

Figure 8 – Eastman 6 inch cutting knife
Also shown with rotary cutter

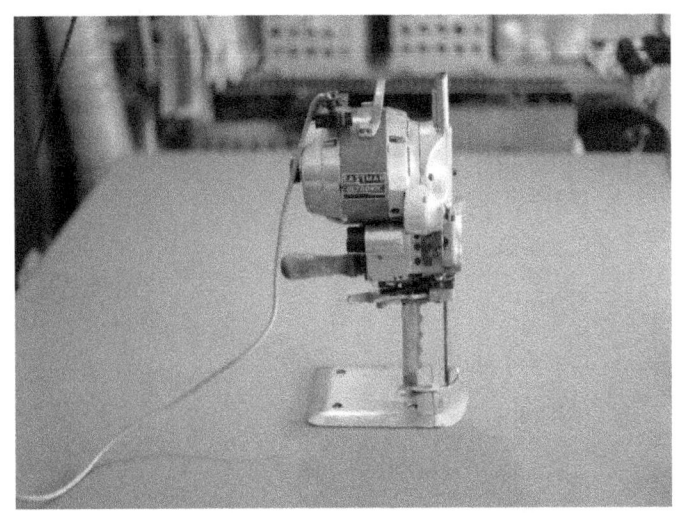

Figure 9 - 6 inch Eastman cutting knife

Chapter Two Summary

Check sheet of supplies and equipment

Straight Stitch Sewing Machine

3 or 5 thread Serger

Shelves

Sewing Room Equipment

Ruler

Hip Curve

French Curve

Tape Measure

Scissors

Cutting Knife

Cutting Table

Chapter Three

Are You My Customer?

The primary function of the marketing plan is to ensure that you have the resources and the wherewithal to do what it takes to make your product work."

---Jay Levinson

Know Your Market! Marketing is the action or business of promoting and selling products or services, the life line of any business large or small is marketing.

Yes I said it marketing. Not your product or your ego, but marketing is the backbone of your business. At the end of the day, marketing is about your target market, engaging them and moving them to action and that action is purchasing your product.

Many of the critical questions that I'm always asked by new designers are, "How do you get the business? How do I get buyers to buy my clothes? How do I get storeowners to pay attention to me?" Those are bona fide questions and I have the answers.

For me the answers didn't come out of a book. It came from sitting down, figuring out who I wanted to sell my product to, how to get in their heads and stay top of their mind so when they were ready to purchase I was the first person they thought of. Since I didn't really consider myself a salesperson, I didn't understand marketing and sales. As a matter of fact I was terrified of sales and shunned it.

What I did understand was pattern drafting and how to sew, so marketing was a new and scary skillset for me. To get people to take note of you, I must admit that you do have to become a bit aggressive. If you're kind of shy, I would suggest taking aggressive pills because you're going to need them or develop mechanisms to help you overcome your fear.

Before you can sell one unit of your product, ask yourself to whom will I sell my product? Many entrepreneurs start spinning their wheels pitching to anyone they think will buy their product. This exercise leads to frustration, unsold product and no cash.

Really it is like your selling yourself cheap just to get a sale. True you may make the sale but did you make a profit? And really what this behavior indicates to the customer is "I don't value myself or my product", so why should they value you? Know your worth and don't cut rate yourself just to make a sale. Everyone is not going to be your customer and the faster you learn that lesson the faster you'll make sales to the right customer.

To sell your product and increase your revenue, you must identify your target audience. Your target audience are the people who will benefit the most from your product or services. Understanding their deep desires and lifestyle is critical to your business. This knowledge is critical because it will be the driving force in your product development and marketing strategy. Your goal is to provide tangible or intangible benefits to solve your customer's problems.

You are the Customer's PROBLEM SOLVER!

Once you fully internalize this concept, you'll look at marketing in a much more insightful way.
For example, when I learned I was a problem solver I began to design clothes that fit better and give the curvy woman a sophisticated elegant look.

In 1992 when I started in the apparel business, I didn't understand marketing. Actually, I thought marketing was simply buying advertising space in the local newspaper and that's not true. What I came to know is marketing is the continuous act of putting your product in front of your target audience. You can use marketing tools like direct mailing, postcards, letters, flyers, email blasts, phone calls, events like fashion or trunk shows are all part of marketing. Notice I didn't say advertisement.

Because you're really in the marketing business, it's important for the fashion entrepreneur to understand the difference. The difference is this. You pay for advertising and it basically is a one shot deal, but marketing is a continuous effort and in many cases little or no money is involved. For example, when an article appeared in a magazine about my label it generated interest in my brand. The interest led potential customers to my website and ultimately converted them into sales.

Many manufacturers or entrepreneurs, like myself, confuse the terms and incorrectly believe that spending money on advertising is marketing.

Advertising is a marketing tool that's at your disposal, but it's not the only tool to use in marketing. **To effectively market, you have to plan,** which means you'll have to build a marketing plan.

What Is a Marketing Plan?

Let's say your goal is to increase revenue by 50%. Ask yourself what are the steps involved to accomplish this task? It's not enough to say you want to increase your business' income, you need a definite plan to increase income, whether you decide to sell direct to the consumer or to boutiques, you need a plan. In my case, and the reason for this book is to explain how to build a plan and one that works for you specifically. What works well for one person may not work well for another; so it's up to you to determine the effort you want to spend on your plan. In all cases you have to bring value to your customer by solving a problem.

What things can you do to build your plan and what tools and components do you need? One easy and low cost thing can do is to host focus groups. That takes a little effort, but in the long run, is definitely worth it.

For the best results, engage no more than 10-15 people so it won't become unmanageable. If you're marketing to women's boutiques, host a tea party or an informal luncheon where you sit down and talk with them. You really do want to know their psyche and the psyche of their customers. Why do they buy certain pieces for their boutique? If you're selling straight to the consumer you want to know why they would buy a red dress versus a pink or a blue dress. Was it the cut, the style, the length? These are questions you need to ask in your focus group. Develop a list of questions ahead of time to ask the group.

If you're selling direct to boutiques, you'll want to visit the stores. Call ahead of time, tell them you're a manufacturer, you'll be in the area and you want to stop in at an appropriate time to say hello and chat with them about their business. You will be pleasantly surprised, to know people will talk to you about their businesses if you show a genuine interest in providing a resolution for their particular problem.

I take a day out of my schedule and go from boutique to boutique introducing my company and spending what I call quality time getting to know each owner and building a relationship with them. I perform this task at least once per week. I take my lunch time or use the early morning hours to go by boutique windows to analyze the merchandising and apparel color scheme.

For those of you who are just starting into the fashion business, I suggest picking one day per week and not a Saturday because store personnel are way too busy, but on the other hand this may be an opportunity for you to view the customers in action. Observer the garments they are picking out. Start a little conversation with them about their choices. I love doing this! This is really a one-on-one survey with the customer.

When targeting a buyer, which in many cases is the store owner, I carry candy, sometimes flowers, but I always leave a business card and take my battery of questions and ask them, "How's business? Their responses vary, from good to not so good. Then I ask what they'd like to improve on and what things they'd like to carry in their store that they find difficult to buy at trade shows? Trust me, they'll open up and tell you. These are key points for you to take home and start your development, because they're telling you exactly what they're going to buy. They'll tell you what they can't find and what they're looking for.

If you can identify something that they aren't finding, then bingo, there's an opportunity for you. It's important to think of yourself as an investigator to determine what your customers want. That's the way I approach it, as if I'm on an investigative mission. Choose your investigation day when you will get out and visit your customers. The other thing this does is put your face and name in front of them. They will recall that you're the lady that stopped by. I'll never forget when I had a customer tell me, "You're the only person that ever called and asked me anything. You're the only person that ever cared."

So what do you ask the potential clients? Here's a short list I developed

I ask questions like --

Who is your clientele?

What are your store's price points?

What are your best selling products?

What items do you find difficult to purchase that your customers want?

What is the lifestyle of your customer?

What trade shows do you attend?

What is that one thing your customers really want that you don't carry?

What brands to you currently carry in your store?

The answers to these questions are the basis for building your product development strategy and marketing plan.

Guerilla Marketing

I turned a corner in my life when I learned about marketing and especially Guerilla Marketing, a book I pulled off the shelf by Jay Conrad Levinson. Reading his book was a life-changing experience because it brought clarity to my disheveled marketing scheme.

I would suggest investing in this book and implementing as much, if not all, that you can. The first thing I did was to print flyers and I actually taped them in women's bathrooms and in office buildings. I got calls, not always nice ones but with persistence you can find places for your flyers that will give you the appropriate response.

Why do we buy? That's a critical question. Why are my customers buying? What's driving them? Paco Underhill, author of "Why We Buy", answers most of those questions. I used a lot of techniques from this book but didn't understand there was a science behind it. How do you find out why people buy? You have to visit the mall, not to go shopping, to use your investigative skills and find out why consumers are buying and why are they going into your soon to be customer's store? What's drawing them? Is it the window? Is there something in the window that's drawing them in? Stand behind the customers and listen to their conversations. What are they talking about? Follow them into the store, careful not to become a stalker!

Stay a good length away but within ear shot, pay attention and take notes. Why did they pick up the yellow blouse with the cute collar? You could engage them in conversation by saying, "I was going to buy that, what do you like about it?" Most often they will tell you.

You can become an asset to the storeowner by telling them, "Your customers told me they like this kind of blouse because........"
I was in a store and happened upon some ladies and we all picked up a blouse.

I was curious and asked them why they put it back. One woman said, "It's not in my size, if they had it in my size I would have bought it." Maybe the storeowner thought they only needed sizes small to large because they're not talking to their customers they missed the sale by not providing product geared to this customer demographic. Remember you are building a long term relationship with the owner and by doing so your resolutions are solving a problem and becoming an asset and ally to that store. Remember this is not about you rather, it's for the store and it indirectly helps you.

Remember it's not about you; it's all about your customer

When we're in the mall watching customers, this is called 'trend shopping'. I didn't learn this until later in business, but I've always been a nosey person, so you'll have to develop your curiosity and become a nosey person too. When I go to the mall I invest in butter pecan ice cream, two scoops, and I sit on a bench, watch people and take notes.
I watch what they're scooping up and eating. I listen to conversations and if I can I will engage them. Watch and learn. How many people go into the store between the hours of 12:00 and 1:00? What happens at 2:00 o'clock? Does the traffic drop off? If so, is it because they're out for lunch and they're trying to buy for a special occasion, or just browsing? Then at 2:00 o'clock what happens? Have those people returned to their offices? You want to be able to answer these questions and keep tabs on how many people are going into the store. If the store has little or no traffic;

then they're definitely not a good candidate for your marketing effort.

I target specific stores based on price point. Price point is the suggest retail price of the product(s) in a store. The category of price points in the retail industry are discount (off price), budget, moderate, contemporary, better, bridge, designer and haute couture. I identify the store by making a phone call and ask what are the store's prices points. If they are within my target range, then they go on the list. If not, I move on. This is a time consuming project but in the long run it will save you aggravation by trying to sell to a store that can't afford your product.

After you've collected the information, you can go into the store and conduct an intelligent conversation with management about your analysis. Tell them you've seen 20 people come in between 12:00 and 1:00, 30 people between 5:00 and 6:00 and 40 people coming in between 6:00 and 7:00. Watch and figure out what the trends are. How many people came out with packages compared to the number of people without packages? That's critical information. It sounds like a lot of work and it is, however, to be successful, you'll have to put in the time.

Armed with this knowledge, you'll be able to talk more definitively at tradeshows about customer problems and how, according to your research, your product solves the problem. When you stand up before buyers who only have five minutes, you can say, "I know how many people go in and out of boutiques and I know this sells and I know this doesn't." If they ask you what stores, you can tell them, "I'm not at liberty to say, but it's one down the street from you."

Now you've captured their attention because they want to know what their competitors are doing. Perhaps their competitors are benefitting from something they could be doing.

You always want to be in the position of 'helping' and providing a benefit. Come with an attitude of solving a problem, one that they don't have time to solve. You have taken the time and you're showing them that you're on the street doing footwork and research to help them. The results of your investigative work can help the store owner by showing them what is trending. They're going to buy from you because:

· You have built a relationship with them

·   You're providing the answers that solve their problem

One of my clients didn't have the right size lingerie in her store. She serviced larger women but couldn't find romantic, sexy, silky lingerie in larger sizes, it just didn't exist. Trashy lingerie exist and we all know that's fun, but the romantic bridal type lingerie did not exist for larger women. That was her problem and an opportunity for me to resolve the issue.

To really be seen as an authority, you'll have to Travel in order to gain knowledge of trends from a variety of regional areas. For example, what may sell well in Chicago will not sell well in Miami.
The art deco colors may not sell well in Chicago until spring and summer, whereas in Miami or California they sell year round. You can't be an armchair fashionista. You need to be out in different cities to look at what's trending in those areas.

If you're on the east coast, you can find inexpensive flights to New York or if close enough you can drive, and go to the garment district, visit major department stores as well as watching street trends. You can check the Internet to find hotels and maybe pair up with another designer and split you travel costs. Be sure to take a pair of sneakers, pack some water or trail mix and hit the streets. Traveling can be fun because you get to meet people, visit different cities and most of all exchange fashion ideas.

Find out what your customers read or watch. Are they reality show people? Do they just read the front page of the paper and then put it down? Are they reading contemporary magazines? You need to understand what your customer is reading in order to pitch the right marketing material to them. You can assume they're on Facebook and other social media platforms, but you might want to ask if they are just to be sure.

Early on while developing my investigative skills, I used to feel like I was invading a person's privacy because I didn't feel like I could walk up and start conversations with people. I've become quite good at it because I've created what I call ice-breaker sentences to start a conversation. If I'm in a store and someone's reading something I'm familiar with I'll say, "That's a cool article, do you like that?" They'll start talking about what they like about it. It's not that you're becoming an FBI agent, you just want to understand more about how people think and what drives them to purchase.

Don't become overpowering but ask questions and then take all the information you've gathered back to your trusty home manufacturing office and start crunching numbers, put it up on a storyboard, tape it to the wall and start looking at trends. What are they talking about? What was the age bracket (demographic)?

Were these women between 45 and 65 or 25 and 45? In the case of women between the ages of 50 and 65, the trend is they're the new 40. They don't want to look like grandmothers. They don't want to look frumpy. They're still very vibrant, active women who have their own businesses, have discretionary income and don't want to look old. That's important to know because when you sit with your design team, this information is the launch pad for product development. You'll realize that not everyone is a size 2 and may have some tucks and rolls; you'll want to address the tucks and rolls in a sexy, flattering and sleek way. This goes back to your design skills where silhouettes come into play.

Early on in my startup, I wanted to understand the plus size market. I didn't have numbers and didn't understand sizing so every day after work I would chase women down the street and tell them they had the perfect body size for my research project. They were flattered. I would promptly take out my tape measure and ask if I could take their measurements. Then we'd step to the side and I would measure the women out on the street. I took the numbers and inserted them into my spreadsheet and then I would go to the next person.

I found the best time to do this was at lunchtime because everyone was out and about, which provided me with more choices of women and they weren't as hurried as they would have been when leaving work.

Surprisingly, I only had one or two rejections out of maybe 100 women. They were very willing because they felt it was important since they wanted trendy and stylish clothes. So, you have to do the same thing, find the perfect body and come up with the perfect pitch to find the answer to your potential customer's problem or desire.

Chapter Three Summary

- Inform the customer why you are conducting research
- Remember you are solving a problem
- Marketing is a constant activity
- Marketing has many tools to accomplish business goals
- Develop a survey of ten questions for your customer base
- Make visits to the end customers
- Cruise the mall and watch customer habits

Chapter Four

How Do I Get the Business?

"I had to make my own living and my own opportunity. But I made it! Don't sit down and wait for the opportunities to come. Get up and make them."
-- Madam C.J. Walker

Madam C.J. Walker, daughter of former slaves was determined to make a way for herself and with hard work and perseverance she built one of the most successful black owned businesses in the early 20th century and became the first woman self-made millionaire in the United States of America. She was a single mom, a low wage laundry worker working sometimes 14 hour days for $1.50 per day. She had some pretty stiff odds stacked against her but she developed a product out of need and knew how to market giving free demonstrations and selling her product door-to-door to friends and neighbors. So out of the depths of poverty and deprivation Madame C.J. Walker lifted herself, so why can't you? There are tons more resources at your disposal to market your product. Let's talk about some of the options I used.

You know I'm a low budget person so these are steps you can use immediately.

So here's my A-list. It is Home Shows, Store Trunk Shows, Presentations, and Industry Trade Shows. I'll start with the easy low cost options and move into the more expensive methods to gain a customer base and grow your business.

Home Shows

One of the easiest and best ways to make sales and test your product is to sponsor home shows. My home shows consisted of giveaways, mini fashion show, food, games and prizes to give the function a fun atmosphere. If I sponsored the showing at my home, I sent an email announcing the date, time and place and prizes to be given away, especially the gift to the person who brought the most people to the show.

I was easily earning $1,000.00 per show with a minimum of up front expenses. I purchased the food and setup a small self-serve buffet. I received referrals, the customers had fun and felt good and couldn't wait to attend my next show.

I always made sure to give a special gift to the person who brought the most people because I wanted to build my attendance for the next showing. So at the next home showing, people where competing with each other to bring the most guest and win the cash prize. After each show I sent a cute thank you card to the guests. This is the easiest low cost way to move product and get your name in front of customers, gain customer loyalty for repeat business and build a dynamic customer list.

How I built My Customer List- Referral! Referral! Referral!

Everyone has a friend or several friends right? So my job was to make my home showings so infectious the friend would tell and invite another friend. Everywhere I went I collected names and email addresses so I could keep in touch with the person.

I sent a monthly e-zine where I listed my favorite customer of the month. I included information about her as well as talked about the various activities of the business.

And I always asked for referrals. I developed a promotional flier and at the bottom of it, I collected contact information and I asked for five names in order for the person to receive a free gift. Works like a charm! Who doesn't want to receive a free gift? It doesn't have to be an expensive gift. Typically I bought items from the Dollar Store to wrap as gifts.

Give Them Something To Talk About

To gain new customers and build your list always give your potential customers something to talk about. The MAGNET-- My magnet was a free pair of my prettiest lace panties. I placed a sign-up form on my website and asked the visitor to sign up to receive a free pair of panties. For the free pair of panties I received valuable contact information to market directly to the customer.

Store Trunk Shows

The next thing you can do to get business is to ask boutiques if you can sponsor a trunk show in their store. Trunk shows are really cool. At the turn of the century there were no boutiques. Salesman had clothes in trunks and they went from town to town, opened the trunks, did a little show, and the women bought. With boutiques, I arrange to bring the collection, they provide the food and the customers and we put on a mini fashion show.

Then the customers buy the clothes and I give the store a percentage of the sales, so it's a win-win situation.

Presentations and Cold Calling

Ugh!! Cold calling conjures up the image of a salesperson on the phone and a gruff voice saying, "I've got something to sell you." Since I'm not that kind of person, I developed my own technique of cold calling. I developed a script for myself but before I delivered my cold call and script I would send the client Godiva chocolate. If it was a lingerie company, I would give them a pair of our laciest, sexiest panties along with the Godiva chocolate and send it.

Then by the time they received the package, I would call and say, "Did you receive the Godiva chocolate with lace panties?" They would say, "Oh, of course." Then I'd say, "Well I'm the lady that sent them to you." Response, "Oh, how nice!"

And that opened the door for me to give my presentation and build a relationship. At that point I would simply ask to come in and chat with them because I had some other things to show them.

You'll notice my tone wasn't aggressive. I was coming to them from the point of communication and relationship building. Peter Koch, the CEO of Balluun, said in a seminar that business people want to start selling as soon as they call, but what you want to do is build a relationship. In order to build that relationship, you first have to introduce yourself, not as a seller, but someone who genuinely wants to help the retailer solve problems.

"How can I help you?" That's the phrase that I start my conversation with. When I cold call, I would ask, "Who's the person in charge?" Then, my next statement is, "I just wanted to ask you a few questions. Do you mind? What are the hardest things to keep in your store?" With this entry, they'll talk to you because you're not selling them anything. Instead you're asking questions to find out what they need help with and determining how you can help solve their problem and bring value to their lives.

One of my very first cold calls was to a small plus size chain store in Birmingham, AL. I called several times pleading with the owner to give me a chance to show my collection. He gave his approval and we set a date and time. At the time I was so broke. Literally, I had enough gas to make the round trip and be on empty when I returned to Atlanta. My mom and I arrived at the store a bit ahead of schedule to setup in the owner's office. I gave my presentation and the owner placed a $5,000.00 order on the spot! I asked for a 35% deposit which he gave to me and the balance due when the shipment arrived. I used the money to purchase fabric, trim and pay my contractors.

That was a huge experience and great for my ego but it doesn't mean every call after that was a positive experience. The lesson for you, the fashionpreneur, is to not give up when a store owner rejects your call or your product. They are not rejecting you or your product. They may not be ready to integrate your product into their store. Is everybody going to talk to you? No! Am I saying that no one's going to abruptly end the phone call? No! What I am saying is that you can minimize the abrupt disconnects by developing pre-call techniques and doing some research to find out the nuances of the targeted stores. I'm still terrified of cold calling as it gives me the willies, but I've learned to grow a little bit thicker skin and developed a technique that minimizes my emotional discomfort.

Networking

Outside of cold calling, it's good to get to know people in the industry. How do you do that? When people say network, what does network mean? How do you network? There are books and newsletters on networking extolling you to be "there". You have to run to every event and push your cards. Really? I don't run to every networking event shake hands and push my business cards. I choose with whom I want to speak and I'm very selective about who I throw the business cards to.

If I go to networking events, I engage people telling them what I do and then ask them how I can help them accomplish what they want to do. I look at it from the point of view of I'm helping you get to where you want to be, and maybe in turn there may be something you know that can help me.

It is not necessary to attend every networking event, but when you do attend an event, you need to strategically work the event. To strategically work an event, decide prior to the date, with whom you want to engage. For example, if you are invited to attend a local networking function, call the sponsor and ask who are the potential attendees and their respective industries. If you are looking for a graphic designer, narrow your list to these groups of names and make them top of your list to meet.

With the age of technology, networking comes pretty easily now because we've got Facebook, Twitter and LinkedIn, but again these should be strategic partnerships. On Facebook, I don't friend everybody. As a matter of fact, if I were going to be judged by how many friends I have, compared to other people, I would certainly lose. You want to friend people that you can help add value to their business and they can help add value to your business. A win-win situation.

If you're using Facebook, use it strategically, aligning yourself with people that are in the industry and people that you can work with successfully. Use Facebook to the best of your ability. Go ahead and set up a Facebook page and a business Facebook page but understand that you're not going to sell from that page. You're going to use Facebook to drive people to your website. This is part of the hustle of getting your name and product out there.

You will also want to have a link on your website back to Facebook. Your website should be sleek and professional so that you can compete with the best of the best.

Originally I sat down and looked at the competition and said to myself, "Who's doing this better than me?" Those are the people I wanted to emulate. Observing what my competition was doing pushed me to be better. Your website, Facebook page, business cards and letterhead should all be in sync with a crisp and professional logo that says you're not some crummy little startup. You want to look as professional as the top name in the industry.

When you're wondering how to get your name out there and what you need to do, think tradeshows. A lot of fashion entrepreneurs coming into the business are terrified by the thought of going to a tradeshow because they're costly. If you're thinking about doing a major tradeshow, you're easily looking at $1,800 - $6,000 for three days of work and you may not write an order. It's been my experience that you will not write an order if you're fresh out on the street because you don't have what they call in the business any creds (credibility). Who knows you? Who have you sold to? Nobody. They're not going to take a gamble on you.

Preparing/Producing for a Trade Show

What do you do to minimize the risk of laying out $1,800 - $6,000 of your hard earned cash and not writing a sales order? What are the steps you need to take? You can partner with two, three or four other designers. Especially if you're considering large scale shows. I will tell you right now that you should do your research before you go for the big gun because you really need to start small and work your way up.

I was given that advice by a Nordstrom's buyer. When I called Nordstrom it was my dream to sell to Nordstrom. I dreamt about it and lived for the day that I could ship to Nordstrom. I had a wonderful conversation with the buyer and told her that I was calling to get information about what I needed to do to sell to her.

The first thing she asked me was, "who are you selling to now?". I took a deep breath and told her I was selling to small mom and pop organizations, one and two chains. She said, "That's good."
She asked me what I produced and I told her. She said, "That's great. I like the fact that you're selling to smaller boutiques. That's good because it gives you practice. I don't think right now you could ship to us, but continue shipping to those smaller stores to get that practice. By the time you come back to us, you'll understand what we require".

I thought that was a good piece of advice. She didn't slam the door in my face and say they would never buy from me, but she was willing to take the time to talk to me and explain Nordstrom's procedure and the best procedure for me. She said the first thing they wanted to know is how many stores I had shipped to. She said when I had increased the number of ship-to stores, then I would be ready to ship to Nordstrom.

We'll talk about Nordstrom a little bit later because there is an interesting way to do business with the larger retailers. If you're at a tradeshow and they happen to come up to your booth, like your goods and want to write a purchase order with you, you'll need a backend operations system to support shipping to thousands of stores weekly. You need to take into consideration they will ask you about your volume output, how many pieces you can produce per week and terms. When I started running production internally, I counted how long it took us to produce a garment and looked for places in the process where I could speed up the output. For large retailers output and speed to market are critical and the pressure is on the manufacturer to meet the store's requirement. Before launching into a relationship with a large retailer, ensure you have the operations capacity for high volume.

Purchase Order

When you attend the tradeshows and thinking about writing orders, depending on the store, understand you have to pay for the order production upfront. In other words, you will have to bear the cost of fabric sourcing and production. Larger retailers work on a terms basis usually a net 30 or 45 days or whatever you and the buyer negotiate.

Understand that you will not receive payment until 30 to 45 days after the ship date.

If you get an order for 1,000 pieces, for example, you source the fabric, the trim, and ship the order. You will not see any money for 30 to 60 days. So be aware, you're going to be out all of that money until they pay the invoice.

The best advice, and what I've learned from experience is to work with the smaller boutiques, ship smaller orders and work on your credibility. When I say credibility, I mean produce quality garments, ship on time and keep your word. If you're having a problem in production, don't be afraid to pick up the phone and say we may have to push the ship date back a week because the material was late in getting to you or something happened. They may scream and yell but integrity counts more than anything.

Develop Your Line Sheet

When attending tradeshows or out conducting research for potential boutique clients, you'll want to have your business card and line sheet in your hand. A line sheet is nothing more than photos of your collection, the style number, the price point and the size of that particular component. It is just flat drawings on paper with your logo, your name and your contact information so the buyer has something in hand if they walk away from you.

Walking the Show

Before you invest in any tradeshow, it's always a good idea to walk the show because every tradeshow may not be right for you depending on what you're producing. When I first started out, I produced unlined suits for larger women. I targeted attorneys, doctors, judges and women who could not go in the store and get classic suits.

I had to find tradeshows with buyers for stores that carried that particular item. To find tradeshows which had exhibitors that carried similar product, I called the show producer and told them I was thinking about coming to their show and I want to walk the show as a guest to observe and discuss the type of clients that frequent the show. Are they high end or mid-range? Is this an off price or discount tradeshow? The producer/coordinator will tell you.

High on the list for review is the size of the show. How many exhibitors attend the show? If the show is produced several times per year, what are the attendee numbers per show? Which show has the highest number of attendees? What exhibitor amenities are provided? Will you be provided attendee contact information for pre-marketing?

Along with show size and attendee numbers, discuss the physical show amenities. A typical booth setup is a carpeted 10 x 10 with a curtain across the back, one table, two chairs, and a trash can. As a vendor, you take your collection and always use nice chrome or wooden hangers. We take our racks, our own sign and banner. To enhance the merchandising experience, we take our own lights and purchase electricity. Most trade shows will provide electricity, racks, lighting, grids, and internet access for an additional fee.

When I walk a show the features I look for are the number of booths and the number and type of buyer attending the show. I look at what's being provided by the producer. Are they giving us the curtain back or is it just a 10 x 10 and nothing else? I look at how many visitors are actually sitting in the booths. Are the exhibitors getting a lot of business or are people just looking? If they're predominantly looky-loos, I don't need to be there. What was the buyer attendance number for the past two to three shows. I actually talk to the buyers to get their opinion of the show and ask how often they attend the show.

Then I look at the competition. What are they selling? Are they selling something that's comparable to what I have or are they selling something completely different than my collection? With the competition in mind, I look for avenues where I can differentiate myself to stand out in the crowd and attract the right kind of customers.

Expense and Energy For A Show

Booth space is currently running anywhere from $1,800 to $6,000 depending on the shows. Keep in mind you have to pay for airfare, food, cab fare, tipping and hotel, plus shipping all your stuff there and back. You'll also need salesmen trunks which are nothing but large luggage on wheels. We also steam everything and make sure the tags are attached to each garment. There's a lot of expense and a lot of energy involved.

The three step process to choosing the right tradeshow is,

1. Conduct research online
2. Talk to show producers
3. Walk the show

As a participant in the International Lingerie Show (Las Vegas), what helped me differentiate myself was walking the show and talking to the producers. The next step is to ask them what they would provide the exhibitors before and after the show. Are they going to provide customer's names and databases? That was critical for me because I knew I wasn't going to write any orders the first time out and it was likely that I wasn't going to interact with a lot of people, so I needed to do some upfront marketing.

I asked the show producer if I bought the booth, would he give me a database of the buyer's names so I could contact them before the show. In some cases show producers will provide contact information. It is important to get that information because it's after the show that you're going to make your sales. You won't make substantial sales during a show until after you've established yourself. To establish yourself with the buyers and other exhibitors, a minimum of three shows seems to be the cross over point from newbie to established exhibitor. I used the database to generate labels and sent out very loud yellow postcards. It was always gratifying to me to see those yellow cards held in the hands of people frantically looking for my booth. This is a simple process that has worked very well for me.

When you exhibit at a tradeshow the key activity is for you to observe, to listen and to ask questions. Questions, questions, questions. If you can get them to stop and come inside your booth, that's half of the sale right there. If they're steadily walking by and you haven't tripped them, you're not going to get in their sight. You have to develop attention grabbing techniques, especially when you're new. Don't feel bad if no one stops at your booth because that's the nature of the business; they're not going to stop. You have to be aggressive and find a way to help them stop.

I developed strategic methods as a way of pulling them in. I use a video on my laptop so they could see the clothes and the lingerie. You can give away gifts. I used to staple candy to my business card and do simple things like that. For a gimmick, since I made large clothes, I made the largest garment I could possibly make and hung it across my booth. People looked at me and this humungous garment and were a bit taken back. They thought it was funny, it got their attention and it got them to stop.

You have to find attention grabbers that work for you. As newbies on the street, I've seen designers cry and become really depressed at tradeshows because buyers would not stop and review their collections. I've felt really bad and wanted to tell them that just because you show up doesn't mean they're going to come to you.

To alleviate some of the first show blues, It's good to engage and build a strong relationship with the show producers and stay in their good graces because they're going to give you a lot of helpful information, like what type of buyers attend their shows and the buyers spending habits. They may not give exact figures but they will tell you a ballpark figure. You can also talk to some of the exhibitors and tell them you're thinking about exhibiting in the show and you want a sense of the pros and cons of the show.

Ask them questions:

1. Ask about the flow of traffic
2. How long have they exhibited at this show?
3. What's the busiest show?
4. How is this show's attendance and buyer's spending compared to previous years.

It's not like you're trying to pry into their world and steal their customers, you just want to know how it's working for them.

As a first time exhibitor, sending post cards, emails and making phone calls prior to the show, will significantly increase your chances of buyers coming by your booth to meet you and talk about your collection. Always make sure you can get their business cards and listen to their suggestions. If a buyer approaches your booth, you can use your pre-rehearsed basic script.

My basic script is, "Hello pleased to meet you. My lingerie collection consist of baby dolls, gowns, teddies and panties, these items range from size large to 5X and they come in four colors". Give them the basics and then ask them what they're looking for. You might ask, "What are the things that you find hard to obtain that you're not seeing at the show? How can I help you? Is there anything you think our company can do to help you with your sales?" When you say that, their ears perk up because they're looking for ways to increase their revenue. It's helpful to both parties, when manufacturers can partner with stores because you can zero in and produce product that works for their store. By establishing a partnership, you're adding extra value from the back end because you're giving them specific pieces rather than a random selection of garments which may or may not integrate with their current product mix.

You can talk about ways to help them and maybe even suggest a private label.

Private label is when you make clothes specifically for a store and apply their label. If that's an option you can exercise, let them know you're available to do that, but there's a criteria they'll have to meet. To do one or two pieces is not worth your effort. Private label is an excellent method of getting into the stores and producing larger volume.

While offering private label and other services, I always ask the buyer for referrals. I've found that buyers have buyer friends and they run in packs. We were at a show in Miami and by day two we hadn't made a sale, but we hadn't given up. Later another exhibitor for another really large line, sat down with us and chatted. He found out what we were doing and said he really liked our line. Then he started flagging down some of the high rolling buyers that he knew personally. These guys had been passing us for two days without stopping. As he invited them in, we started conversations and started making sales. We met one particular buyer from a high end men's store in Las Vegas, who liked my pink satin shirts. He said,

"You should go around the corner and look at the suit colors produced by a popular exhibitor because those were the colors I need". He asked to start with a minimum order which I was happy to write. Then he called over his friend who had been walking up and down that aisle for two days without stopping.

These guys started buying from me. I shipped the order and they loved the pink satin shirts but thought they were rather pricey. My response was that they're pricey but very high quality. He said his customers really liked them so when he reordered, I was curious and asked who was wearing a 3X pink satin shirt. He said his customers were flamboyant football players and wrestlers. When I asked how many more pink satin shirts he needed, he asked if I could make them larger. He really liked our product and though he complained about the price, I stood my ground and didn't lower my price. They were pricey but we added value to those garments by putting in very thin stitching on the cuffs and collar and our buttons were exquisite.

I ended up producing the shirts in pink, lavender and green satin. This is when I thoroughly comprehended marketing is all about the customer and not me.

Credit or No Credit

You have to decide before you go to the show whether you're going to offer credit or no credit. In the U.S. market for the bigger stores the way goods are paid for is on credit terms. Be sure to check the creditworthiness of the company interested in purchasing from you. I ask for three references and call the sources and ask about the potential client's payment history.

Just because they may have a high profile brand name doesn't ensure they are credit worthy. They may be a popular store but will be a huge headache for you by not paying their bill on time or at all.

I've had this happen and was strung out for almost 90 days. This is a situation where you become a credit collector and I'm not in the credit collecting business. There are companies, known as factors, that will loan you money based on your purchase order and will help you get the orders started.

Early on I gave customers credit terms of 30 days to pay for their goods. As things went along buyers weren't able to pay on time and the system didn't work well for me. I can't afford to give credit. So if they're demanding that I give them credit, then they're not going to be my customer unless I use a factor and the potential customer has a strong credit history. You have to be able to foot the bill before you get paid up to 30 days after the ship date and in many instances the waiting period diminishes cash flow.

To check the person or the store's creditworthiness, you can call credit collectors or you can arrange to have their credit checked. Ask them for references and who they have done business with at the show. Ask other exhibitors at the show about the potential client. When you speak to other exhibitors or call their references ask questions such as:

1. Do they pay their bills on time?
2. Have they ever been late?
3. How long was it, 30, 60 or 90 days?

If you don't feel that you can do business with the store on a credit basis, then don't start the order. Don't feel pressured to write the order in desperation. We finally got to the point where we said it's a minimum amount placed on their store or buyer's credit card.

Macy's Minority Diversification Program

Another way you can get your name out there and get business is through Macy's Minority Diversification Program. You can go to their website at:*http://www.macysinc.com/businessfashion/workshop/.* The Workshop at Macy's is a comprehensive retail vendor development program designed to educate, prepare, and mentor high potential multicultural and/or women-owned business owners on how to perform and sustain growth in the retail industry. They offer a course, 4 1/2 day sessions, teach minority and small female-owned firms how to break into working with Macy's. In May 2011 with an inaugural class of 20 vendors, The course taught by industry experts, focuses on strategic planning, branding, sales and marketing, financial management, assortment planning, merchandising, and access to capital which are critical pieces in order to be a successful vendor within the Macy's supplier channel. Macy's took the initial step to launch this program with the ultimate goal of being the benchmark for retail supplier diversity.

Chapter Four Summary

- Money generating methods
- Home Trunk Shows
- Store Trunk Shows
- On-line stores
- Trade Shows
- Build and use you referral list

Chapter Five

Down In the Trenches

"The ultimate measure of a man is not where he stands in moments of comfort and convenience, but where he stands at times of challenge and controversy."
-- Martin Luther King, Jr

Pattern Development, Samples and Pre-Production

When you first start the design process, you're going to begin with a sketch of an idea that was conceived in your mind. It was a fleeting idea but you jotted it down in your sketchbook before it escaped, next step is to turn the sketch into reality or your finished garment. You may not have pattern making skills but you're passionate about the fashion industry and know you want to be in the business. So what are the next steps? Ultimately, you have two options; you can either make the pattern yourself or you can contract the task out to a professional pattern maker. Either way, you need to understand the concept of pattern making and the terminology.

When I first started in the fashion industry, I possessed basic sewing skills, but I really didn't have any of the technical skills to develop a pattern using flat pattern techniques. Flat pattern technique is the technical process for developing garment patterns for use in production. For sample and production garments, stylized patterns are made from a foundation pattern called a sloper (home sewing term) or block (industrial production term).

To gain the flat pattern knowledge, I hired the services of a designer to guide me through the training process. However, to be a fashion entrepreneur, you don't need to know how to sew or make patterns, these services can be outsourced to a contractor, but it is helpful to have some working knowledge of pattern development, design techniques and industry vocabulary in order to communicate design and production information accurately.

A contractor or freelance pattern maker can be found through several sources. Those sources are advertisement in your local paper, contact fashion design schools, craigslist, industry trade journals, yellow pages of your phone book, and sewing guilds. My recommendation is to use industry trade journals. Once you settle on a form of attracting potential pattern makers, I suggest interviewing several contractors versus going with the first choice. During the interview process, go to their shop or studio so you can look at the facility. Take notice if they have suitable clean work areas and tools of the trade. I once interviewed a young woman to make samples for me. Upon arrival at her comfortable and neat family home, I asked what type of machine she used to make her garments and the answer to that question was a muddled assortment of responses.

She refused my request to see the machine or her work area so I became suspicious. The next set of questions concerned turnaround time for the garment. This situation didn't turn out very well because I couldn't inspect the work area and the potential contractor's inability to give a stated completion date for the items. Caution: if you don't see the work area and the tools don't contract with the person. **BIG RED FLAG**!

If you decide not to contract the pattern development work to a contractor and want to keep the work in-house, decide how you are going to acquire the knowledge. Will it be through a formal training course, workshop or hire a private tutor? Whichever method you choose, include the time needed to acquire the skill into your overall plan to launch your collection.

My pattern development training was a two year intensive process under the guidance of my instructor. During that two year period I learned the techniques to bring my fashion ideas to life. To take my idea from paper to garment, I start by drafting my pattern using what is called trash paper, a translucent thin throwaway paper that's yellow or white, easily purchased at an art or craft store. I draft on trash paper first before putting it on oak tag, paper similar in weight to poster board, so I can easily make style modifications. Oak tag is reserved for the perfected and final version of the pattern. If you make a mistake on the trash paper you can erase and start again, but once it's on oak tag, you can't crumple it up or erase it. From my experience, my suggestion is to start with trash or drafting paper for the first part of your pattern making.

But wait - before you can draft a pattern you need measurements! How do you get the measurements? Measurements or specifications are industry standards published for each apparel category. You can easily find your particular industry measurements via your favorite search engine. But if you want accurate measurements, take the measurements from a live person - your fit model.

A fit model is a person used to check the fit, drape and visual appearance of a design. Additionally, the person becomes a part of the design process by providing objective feedback regarding feel of the fabric against the skin and fit of the garment.

"An expert fit model, or even an advanced fit model, knows the problems before they happen. They know how your sleeve should fit, how the material will react to the body, how the buttons should be, how the stitching should be and that's what sells the garment."

---Susan Levine MSA Models- New York.

Since I'm in the plus size industry, let's consider how a fit model can make a garment marketable.

After pattern development and the first sample is made, I ask my sample size fit model to try on the garment. The fit model will tell me how the garment feels against her skin. Items she'll comment on are the fit of the garment and its general appeal. In the case of pants, she'll tell me whether the rise, the measurement from the navel through the crotch to the back waistline, is comfortable. I check the drape of the garment, button placement and neckline.

In the plus size industry we're not quite standardized and I've actually developed my own standard numbers after years of measuring women on the street, using fit models and facilitating focus groups to collect size information. My numbers run pretty much in tandem with what's called "industry sizes", but the one nagging problem in the plus size industry remains fit. Here's an example, the normal size bicep is between 14 -17 inches, however in most ready-to-wear garments the sleeve area is too tight. A second example is the waist area. The assumption is made that if the woman is "big" then she's big all over. Plus size women have definition! Among the design community, the big thing I've found is that many designers tend to use standardized grading rules rather than live fit models that are representative of the average woman. Using a live fit model helps with the design process by giving a visual guideline to understanding the body. You have to understand the body; there's no way around that fact. In order to understand the body types, you must have a **live** model to try the clothes on so you can view the drape of the garment and make corrections if necessary.

In order to make sure your sample size is a good fit you have to use a 'test pattern' to true up the garment. When I test or true a pattern, I sew a sample garment in muslin similar to the weight of the fashion fabric. To true a pattern means to check for the following items:

- Ensure seam alignment
- Sleeve fits armhole

- Sleeve length
- Finished garment length is even
- Evenness of the hem
- Button placement (no gaps between buttons)

After the first sample garment is sewn, try it on a fit model, and check for accuracy using the check sheet above. If all is good, cut and sew the final sample which is called 'the salesman's sample. You've made all the corrections in your pattern, but this time you're going to sew the garment in the fashion fabric the way it's going to look when a salesman presents it or if you present it during a presentation at a trade show. It will have all the corrections made, the selected trim, the selected buttons and the desired hem length according to your specifications.

When the salesman sample is finalized, copy the paper pattern on to oak tag and mark your grain lines on the pattern, which show that it is going to be cut on the bias or on what's called the straight grain. The grain lines and style number, to identify the garment, need to be marked on all pattern pieces.

I want to stress here, once the patterns are finalized and approved, these will be your production patterns. All changes are halted! NO CHANGES in production! This is why you test your garments so any discrepancies can be captured and corrected.

You don't want to make changes in production because it wastes a lot of time and money; not to mention the frustration and ill feeling you cause with the sewing staff and you really don't want to tick them off! Trust me. I've messed up production so bad they almost called for a mutiny. Stay with the final patterns and organize them by categories.

So how do you determine the categories? Determining style categories is fairly simple. Start by developing a style number system for the types of garments you plan to produce.

In the beginning my number system was all over the place and whatever I thought up at the time worked. For example, one season the styles were 1010 then I'd forget what I'd assigned to the group and give it a different number. We were always in a state of confusion and chaos. We just knew styles by shape and a few scribbled notes. This haphazard approach wasted valuable time because the staff couldn't find the patterns, and so matching pattern pieces was a nightmare. Not to mention it drove the staff and me crazy! Then by a stroke of good wisdom, one late night as I was preparing a collection,

I put them into categories and voila; life became much easier.

This made sense and resonated with me. Why I didn't think of this before – I don't know. So I hope you'll take a big hint from me and set your categories before you sketch or sew anything.

Here's what I came up with.

Category Name	Style Number Group
Dresses	1000
Skirts	1100
Tops	2100
Pants	3100
Jackets	4100

Each time I develop a new dress I just add a number. So my first dress would be 1000 and the next style would be 1001, and so on. A system like this will help you keep track of your different type of designs for clarity and continuity. I can't emphasize this component enough, make sure you take care of this process early on to avoid financial pitfalls and insanity.

The process may seem somewhat time-consuming, and it is, trust me, but in the long run it will make a huge difference in production. For one, your production process will flow efficiently because the patterns are labeled and easy to find.

At this point you're ready to write the specifications for your garment. Technical specifications or Tech pack is a document that contains all of the construction details of a garment.

In large companies the designer, in collaboration with the merchandiser develops the documentation. After finalizing the document, the garment and technical specification is sent to the sample room in order to produce a sample run of one or two dozen garments. This final step before production, is important because the sample sewing operators will determine if the details and the actual sewn garment are in synch. If they are, the garment is ready for production.

Small operations like myself use the cutting instructions or job card issued to production as the tech pack. I know you are thinking this is a headache and you're right because it's tedious and time consuming but oh so worth it. It's a simple process, really. All you're doing is laying a garment flat on a table, taking a tape measure and measuring your finished shoulder length, armhole, neck opening, sleeve length, button placement(if any), and garment length.

There are two measurements, the finished and the unfinished but what you're measuring right now is the finished garment.   Unfinished garment details are width of seams, length of straps, whether to serge and turn a hem or blind hem. Let's say you have a simple blouse that's t-shirt weight with a V-neckline and it has short sleeves. If you're sending this out to the cutter, be sure to give the measurements of the sleeve length, the armhole measurement, width of the neck and shoulder, width of the bust size across the front, and if it stops at the hip, give the cutter the measurement from side to side, and include how long the garment should be. These are the basics, but depending on the complexity of the garment you're going to give the details, such as tucks or pleats measurements, collar width top stitching, etc. Let's say you cut a blouse pattern out that is 10" wide, but by the time you finish, it may be 8 or 6" wide including the tucks or pleats. These are the type of details you indicate to the pattern and sample maker within your garment specifications.

There are valuable on-line resources which demonstrate how to develop technical specifications or tech packs or you can outsource this task to a contractor. The choice is yours.

Fabric Sourcing

So you have these wonderful beautiful ideas swirling about in your head, as beautiful as they are, you are going to need fabric to bring the ideas to life. So as a small cut and sew operation, where do you go to find fabric? Determining how and where to purchase fabric is called fabric sourcing.

You will hear this term bantered around a good deal in the industry and by exhibitors at trade shows. So when asked where are you sourcing your fabric? The real question being asked is "Where are you buying your fabric?" In this section I discuss how to source fabric as a small business without going crazy.

Start sourcing the fabric, thread, trim, and whatever goes into the particular garment early on in the process. How early? Using my mood board, I source when my sketches are finalized. A mood board is a tool used by designers to help them get a good idea of what their clients are looking for. Mood boards are basically collages of items such as photographs, sketches, clippings, fabric swatches and color samples.

If you're sourcing domestically and just starting out, you can go to tradeshows and seek out fabric suppliers who will sell to you in smaller lots. Most fabric suppliers will demand 100 yards, but if you don't need that quantity, ask if they can supply in smaller amounts. While searching through the tradeshows, be honest and tell them if you need smaller quantities and ask for their minimum order quantity or MOQ. If they say I can't do anything less than 1,000 yards ask if they know vendors who specialize in small quantities. The best one stop shop for sourcing fabric is dgexpo (dgexpo.net) with shows in San Francisco, New York and Miami. DGexpo features a two day textile and trimmings exhibit for designers who have low minimum requirements.

Before you get to the tradeshow, determine your usage, how much fabric will you need for the production run. Let's say you're making one dozen skirts, you know the finished length will be 36" (38 inch unfinished allowing for a 2 inch hem) and they are 40 inches (unfinished) wide at the hip level. To accommodate your pattern pieces 45 or 54 inch fabric will be perfect. Allowing ¼ yard for the waistband you'll need roughly 15 ¾ yards. I typically add 5 yards for production mistakes and mishaps. Rule of thumb – it is better to have more than not enough!

Armed with this information you can then set out to seek suppliers who can meet your demands. However, if you're unable to attend a tradeshow, you can investigate online sources and view their offerings. The businesses that sell small quantities are called converters. Converters take huge amounts of yardage from the fabric manufacturers and turn it into smaller lots for resale. For example, they may get 10,000 yards of denim and divide it into 100 yard rolls, which is more palatable for a small vendor unless you're planning a huge run. As a new fashion entrepreneur, you may only need 25 or 35 yards or so, finding and working with a converter will take care of your needs.

The Internet is a great research tool so use it as your first source and if you can't find what you're looking for then use the phonebook. If you still can't locate what you want start asking fabric suppliers if they have a friend or resource that will sell smaller lots. If you're an ambitious fashion designer and think you need to go overseas, that opens up a whole new and challenging world. It's a fun world and sometimes rather challenging, but you must be emotionally ready for the roller-coaster ride. To find sources, you can use websites like Alibaba.com, fibre2fibre.com, and tradekey.com, which is one of my favorites but you need to be careful because some of the companies on these sites are traders and not manufacturers. The traders are front men for the mills. Simply put, the trading company buys out overruns and end-of-run lots from the mills and resells them.

During one of my several trips to China, when I've tracked down people on Alibaba and arrived at their offices, it was nothing more than an office with samples spread out across the tables and a laptop.

Because they weren't the manufacturers they were just buying lots from manufacturers and selling them online. If they are a trader, ask them if they are able to re-supply a particular dye lot in 100 yards if you need 100 extra yards. Clarify if you will get 100 yards with that same dye lot. If they hesitate, then you need to walk away because they are only traders and they've just bought remnants to sell.

If you prefer not to work domestically, then it's out of your armchair because working overseas can't be done from the Internet. You'll have to be on the ground going from factory to factory, it's tiring, challenging and sometimes frustrating. People will tell you yes we can do it, but then cannot deliver. If you're just starting out, you are better off attending tradeshows in places like Shanghai or Guangzhou and seek out manufacturers, and then start working your way out to the areas in south China where the textile cities are located.

If you're traveling and sourcing overseas it is best to have a check sheet with you. There are specific questions to ask about re-ordering, the minimums and the dye lots, because it's one thing for you to buy 100 or 200 yards of fabric, sew and sell it to a boutique; then if they re-order you can't get the same dye lot to replenish the order --- that's a problem. This can become a huge headache and be very embarrassing.

I had a wonderful upscale boutique in Cleveland to whom we sold a beautiful garment. The owner just loved, it sold well and she re-ordered. I nearly died when I called the fabric source to re-ordered fabric. Imagine my alarm when I learned they had changed the dye lot as it was a shade darker than the original purchase. Dye lots are everything and this goes back to production planning -- make sure you have calculated how much fabric you're going to need for your production run. As I stated earlier, I buy extra fabric as a hedge against production mistakes and emergencies. Keep in mind it's not a perfect world and mistakes do happen in production. If I've calculated 250 yards of material for a particular run, I buy an extra 50 yards just to make sure I have enough fabric to cover any production errors that may occur.

Case in point, we made a beautiful line of moderate unlined suits. They were adorable and we made them in three colors, black, navy blue and beige. We were selling them to boutiques like wildfire. In the middle of production we cut the suit sleeve with both fabric pieces right side up instead of face-to-face and the result was two left sleeves. O-M-G!!

I panicked because I knew we didn't have enough fabric to make up for the mistake. Luckily, we did have some extra cut pieces that had been thrown in the salvage bin and we had just enough width so we could re-cut the sleeve to fix the problem.

> **LESSON LEARNED**
> **Don't cut corners with the fabric!**

The lure of cheap prices without proper preparation can sink your collection. My advice is source domestically until you build your business to a level that warrants your migration to off-shore sourcing. Source domestically as much as possible, use the converters, use the tradeshows and get plenty of experience before you branch out. Save your money and put it back into your business because overseas they are going to hold you to higher minimums than what you would get here in the states.

Sure the prices may be cheaper than domestic fabric but you'll have to cover the cost to ship it back to the U.S. in the event you aren't going to make the garments in the overseas facility.

Even if you have the garments made in an overseas facility, bear in mind the smaller production cost will be higher, in addition to freight cost and other fees which impact the wholesale price to your customer. In the current climate most freight forwarders aren't willing to ship smaller components, even if its air shipment they don't want anything to do with it.

I'm not saying overseas production cannot be accomplished, because it can, but if you're new to the business of fashion, my best advice is to cut the hassle, challenge, headache and excess grey hairs out of your life now and focus on building your wholesale customer base and plan for future growth – but start domestically.

Initially, it's better to source domestically in order to maintain control of the supply process, the turnaround time and access to the manufacturer or supplier versus conducting business remotely via email, snail mail or skype.

Sourcing fabric is one of the early steps in the product life cycle. After fabric sourcing, pattern and sample development, next step is to develop a standard operating procedure (SOP) for production. What I put in my SOP manual are the specific garment manufacturing steps such as which components are constructed first, seam allowances, finishing techniques, embellishments if any and joining procedures. I have a section in my manual for each garment type produced.

Working with a senior sewing operator, we determined the garment construction flow for production; how we were going to put it all together and in what sequence. To determine the sequence, we cut and sewed the garment after which we analyzed the construction steps and documented them. If you produce a run for a season and record the procedure, two seasons later if you want to revisit the style and update it, the documentation eliminates the need to start from the beginning in order to determine the construction steps. We used to waste so much time trying to remember the sewing nuances and precise construction steps we should have written down the first time. My SOP includes how-to-sew sections for each garment and I have a measurements tab and any other kind of special documentation concerning a particular production run.

For example, for our elastic waist skirts, each waist size, 18 - 24, I have to know the exact cut of the elastic so my calculation is to take the waist measurement and subtract two to three inches from the waist which gives me the cut for the elastic. I made a chart for that particular cut so we didn't have to keep scratching our heads and wondering what the elastic size would be for a particular sized skirt measurement. It was always precise and we didn't have to worry about variation. Stores are picky about garment variations. I've had instances where buyers would say "this skirt seems to be a little smaller than the lot you sent before". That's because we've probably forgot what we cut the time before, so to avoid that embarrassment make a chart and put it in your SOP manual.

Another helpful tip is to keep my supplier contact names and numbers in a convenient binder for easy reference. In fact, I actually made a separate binder for my suppliers so when I was ready to re-order I knew where to go to get my supplier information and that includes the contact's name, phone number, etc. I staple a sample of what I bought from that supplier and I write down the style number or material number so when I call them I can say I want to re-order style number XYZ which I ordered from you six months ago. That helps them to help you versus calling and saying you don't remember exactly what you ordered. Disorganization contributes to wasting time and falling behind if you have to get a particular order out of the door. You may have given yourself only 8 to 10 weeks and now you've lost a week or two trying to figure out what you need to do.

Labels

Early on determine what type of name labels to use for your garment either printed or woven. Printed labels are less expensive but I would suggest using woven because the rich texture adds value to your garments. Woven labels will cost a little more, somewhere around $600 for 5,000 labels, but it gives class and sophistication to your garment. Again, you can use the Internet to research label manufacturers.

You can go to tradeshows and speak with sales representatives about their stock, setup and shipping. Of course it's easier to go with a printed label, but it just doesn't look as sophisticated or professional and you want to be known as a supplier who adds value to the store's business.

After determining the label fiber content, you'll need to print care labels, size labels and your name label. To determine what your care label will communicate to the customer, you need to know the content of the fabric and laundering instructions. Let's say your garment is co 50/50 cotton poly blend.

What we do is test the fabric by washing and pressing it and I do this at least two or three times to see if it's going to fade. These are the kinds of things you will need to know in order to give valuable information to customers and position yourself as an authority within your apparel category. Questions to ask yourself to determine the content of your care label are - Can you tumble dry? Should you put it in the dryer or should it be dried on the line or sent to cleaners only? If your garment is cleaners only that needs to be specifically printed on the label, because you don't want the boutique sending it back to you saying our customer came in and complained because she washed the garment in her washer and it fell apart. If you feel that it is necessary to say, "do not wash with bleach", then put it on the care label and any other helpful care tips that you feel need to be communicated to the consumer. For my garments I initially printed separate care, size and name labels, but to cut down on the cost of printing; I combined the care and size label content into one label.

While you're conducting pre-production planning, you'll also need to determine how you're going to ship and what types of packaging you will need. Will you put it on hangers? If so you'll have to invest in those. Or, will you fold them and put them in plastic packaging to ship in boxes or containers? That's something you need to think through because packaging adds to the overall garment cost. If you're just going to fold it and put it into plastic then, find a supplier that can give you a good price on the various types of plastic bags that are available.

Our customers always praise the neatness of our packaging upon arrival at their stores. The comment was made so many times that it prompted me to ask what the other suppliers were sending. The buyers told us other suppliers simply throw the garments in a box and ship them with a packing slip. It takes extra time, but we do press, fold and repress before packaging and placing the finished garment in the shipping cartons. The extra step in the presentation adds value to your garment, your company's image and fosters repeat business.

Chapter Five Summary

- Decide if you or a contractor will develop your patterns
- Source your fabric from suppliers with low minimums
- Always purchase extra fabric in case of emergencies
- Use a live fit model to perfect your garment
- Choose eco-friendly packaging

Chapter Six

Planning and Production

Getting It Done

What do I mean getting it done? What are the steps to production? The first thing you want to do is develop a production plan. What is the plan? The plan is what is known as production planning which means organizing the flow of work to be completed.

The work for production is:
- Spreading and cutting the fabric
- Determining number of cut pieces
- Determine fabric usage
- Calculate resources needed to run production

These are questions you have to think through with production planning in order to have a smooth operation. If you're a small business owner working from your home, you are the production planning manager. As manager, you are going to determine the answers to all of the questions above and more. When you organize, you're organizing two things human resources and tangible goods.

The tangible goods are the fabric, the interfacing that goes along with it, trim, buttons and matching thread. Matching thread is important because down the line, you don't want mismatched thread on the garment which devalues your garment. This may seem trivial, but it happens and you don't want to find out about it at the end of quality control. While in the planning phase ensure you have enough of the correct color thread. Nothing is worse, than not enough of the right color thread. White and black are not a problem, but if you're sewing fuchsia or turquoise and you run out of the shade or the color of thread, that's an issue.

And then there's coordinating workers. How many workers are you going to need? How do you know who you're going to ask? Are you going to need more straight stitch workers? Are you going to need more sergers or people to run the serging machine? The decision depends on the number of items that you're going to sew. That's how you find out how many people you're going to need. I don't have a hard and fast rule for the calculation.

There's not a simple calculation that says if I have this much fabric, I'm going to need this many workers because it depends on their skill set and speed. If it's a simple skirt, you can probably get away with maybe two or at the max three people. So, if you're producing 144 skirts and you've got two weeks to get it out, that's simple. The more complicated the piece, the more people you're going to need with specialized skills.

Let's talk about organizing the actual production run. We decided how many people we're going to need and we also talked about why we're going to need that number of people. Let's talk about checking machinery and organizing components. Let's say we're going to sew a button down blouse with a collar. The small components would be the collar and the cuff on the sleeve. Count all of the components and divide them into groups, large pieces and small pieces.

A standard rule of thumb is to always prep your small pieces first. Once your large and small components are organized determine who will sew designated pieces.

A procedure check sheet should encompass how many workers you're going to need, list the components, how many you're going to cut and check the thread, trim and all the pieces and accessories that you're going to need.

The Cut Sheet or Cut ticket

The cut ticket or sheet is a list of pattern pieces to be cut. Easy right? Logical, right? All of sudden I was overwhelmed again. I say again because running production and figuring out what to do without a "How To" manual was extremely challenging and I always seemed to be in a state of "anxiety". So how do we determine what we're going to cut? After I calmed down, I sat quietly at my desk and thought about the task ahead. I had to develop a way to communicate to the cutter what was in my head. To communicate my thoughts, I prepared what is known in the industry as the infamous cut sheet.

I didn't know about a cut sheet and had never heard of a cut sheet in my life. I was doing all this because I saw a need, I wanted to fill it and I believed I could do it. I didn't have all the resources but I believed in myself and pushed forward.

Not knowing I needed a cut sheet, I took a piece of paper and a ruler and drew what came to be known as a cut sheet. The components on the cut sheet will be the colors and sizes for production. In the vertical column, I listed the colors. Let's say we're going to cut four standard colors, black, white, sea foam green, and lavender. On the horizontal axis, I list the production sizes. In this example they are 12,

14, 16, 18, 20 and 22. I prepared a sample cut sheet to illustrate how to develop it.

Sample Cut Sheet – Style 1003

Color/Size	12	14	16	18	20	22	Total
Black	1	1	3	3	3	1	12
White	1	1	3	3	3	1	12
Sea Foam Green	1	1	3	3	3	1	12
Lavender	1	1	3	3	3	1	12
Total	4	4	12	12	12	4	48

In this example I'm going to cut a total of 48 pieces of style 1003. Since it is one garment I'm going to lay 3 ply or layers for sizes 16, 18 and 20. If you'll notice the size is across the top and the color is in the side column.

Keep in mind there are various methods to develop a cut ticket, where some are extremely complex and others extremely simple like my example.

The point is for you to have a starting point. I work backwards to determine how many pieces to cut per size. In this example, I want a total of 48 pieces. From historical sales data I know the popular selling sizes are 16, 18, and 20. Therefore, I want more of those sizes and less of size 12, 14 and 22. The total for the colors are 1 dozen each. So I'll have a yield of 1 dozen garments in black, white, lavender and sea foam green or a total of 48 pieces. Across the sizes in this example, I'll have a yield of 4 for sizes 12, 14, 22 and 12 for sizes 16, 18, and 20 for a combined total of 48.

If the horizontal and vertical columns total numbers don't match, you've not calculated the size/color amounts correctly. This is simple to fix by reviewing your math and increasing or decreasing your numbers.

In the early stages, it wasn't easy to learn this procedure. I didn't understand the concept. I'm telling you, you can't live without a cut sheet. Keep your cut sheet in your standard operating procedure manual because you're always going to need a hard copy of it on hand whenever you start planning your production.

So now that you have your cut sheet/ticket, you can spread and stack your fabric and of course you have sturdy commercial tables or tables big enough that can handle 60 or 72 inch width fabric. Subsequent to preparing your cut sheet, you can start spreading which means rolling the fabric out to the length that you're going to need to cut the garments.

Here's an interesting trick of the trade. The first contractor I worked with told me I was killing myself, which I was because I didn't understand what I was doing. I was making things more difficult than they really needed to be. So on to the trick of the trade explanation. Let's say you need one and a half yards of fabric to cut a skirt. You roll out one and a half yards and you need 10 layers or ply, that's 10-ply, so you roll that amount, 1 ½ yards, 10 times. I used to roll the whole thing out, measure out a yard and a half and cut it. No, that's not how it's done. She, my loving contractor, taught me to measure out a yard and a half and mark the point on my table using my white grease pencil. From then on you just roll out the fabric to the white chalk mark and cut. You do this step as many times as you need to in order to compile the layers for cutting.

Remember this trick because if you don't, you're going to waste a lot of time and become fatigued. If you don't have a spreading machine, ask another person or two to assist with the spreading.

To help me speed up the process, I started marking various yardage in grease pencil on my cutting table. For example, I would mark 1 ½ yards in white and put a piece of masking tape at the mark. Next I would mark 2 ½ yards using my grease pencil and mark it with masking tape as well and write 2 ½ on it. These are little tricks that you can do to make your life easy, and marking yardage lengths on your table for reference is one of them that really saved me a lot of headache and saved my arm muscles too.

Next stack the fabric in an even pile ensuring all wrinkles are smoothed out and lay your garment pieces on the fabric. In big manufacturing companies, when I was traveling around and watching this procedure, I saw that they used markers. If you're new to the industry, markers are your pattern pieces drawn on paper that you can use to lay on top of the stacks. In the old days, because we made our own patterns, we didn't have a marker so we drew the pattern pieces on the fabric and cut.

That's kind of risky because if you draw it incorrectly and it's not the right piece, the black mark is going to come through. If you trace the pieces on paper and calculate it out, your life will be so much easier. What I do now is spread a piece of paper over the top of the fabric, staple it down and then draw my pieces on it.

Once the marker is complete, write the style number, the name of the component piece (sleeve or front blouse), how many should be cut and any other information you need to convey to the cutter. Sometimes there are pieces that you only need to cut once, but some pieces need to be flipped over and cut twice. This information needs to be noted on the pattern piece to avoid confusion and mistakes. Now you're ready to cut.

If you're a small businessperson, a fashion entrepreneur, you're the person wearing many hats. You're the production planning manager, supervisor and the cutter. Functioning as the cutter, one of the decisions you will make is what cutting tool to use for your production job. For larger jobs 10-ply or more a cutting knife is ideal. If the job is less than 10-ply a rotary cutter will suffice. As you cut your pieces stack them at the end of your cutting table for bundling.

Many emerging designers don't know the bundling process unless they've worked in a factory. In the event you are going to run production in your facility and are not sure about the bundling process ask a veteran contractor to explain the process. If you are going to cut your garments and contract the work out to a production house, the contractors will ask if your work is bundled when they take on the job. In the beginning I didn't know what they were talking about. They looked at me as if to say, "What is your problem?" My problem was lack of knowledge and unfamiliarity of fashion terminology.

Fortunately, some really kind people helped me out. I found a wonderful gentleman in the North Hills of Georgia in Cartersville named Jim. When I had larger jobs to run I would drive up and take my rolls of fabric to Jim's Cut and Sew. I don't know if Jim is still in business now but he was a really good cutter. He was very precise and he knew how to save fabric. He was a retired gentleman and running the cut and sew operation at his leisure out of a shed in the back of his house. Jim would ask how many pieces I needed and when I needed it. Jim would call me when he was finished cutting and I'd drive up, pay him, stack the bundles in the car and drive back to Atlanta.

At that point I had no clue about the nuances of cutting, marking or bundling. I took a keen interest in Jim's work especially spreading fabric, cutting and bundling. He was kind enough to teach the terminology, organization, fabric allocation, fabric usage and bundling. I am so grateful to him for his kindness.

"Bundling" is the process of assembling cut pieces for production in lots grouped by garment size, color, and number of garments. There are a variety of bundling methods depending upon the need, with four basic systems being the most common among manufacturers:

- Item bundling - all pieces that comprise a garment are bundled together.

- Group bundling - several (10-20) garments are put together in a bundle and given to a single operator or team to sew.

- Progressive bundling - pieces corresponding to specific sections of the garment (such as sleeves or a collar) are bundled together and given to one operator. Other operators sew other parts of the garment, which are then assembled into the finished garment in the final phase.

- Unit production system (UPS) - individual garment pieces are delivered to sewers using a computerized, fully mechanized "assembly line" that runs throughout the manufacturing facility. Using a UPS computer monitoring system, a manufacturer can fully track the production of a garment, identify where sewing slowdowns are occurring, and reroute garment pieces to other sewers who work more quickly. Gerber Garment Technology Inc. manufactures a UPS system, which eliminates the need for passing apparel piece bundles from worker to worker. This lowers labor costs because employees spend less time handling bundles and more time sewing. It also facilitates short-cycle manufacturing.

- ☐ Modular or "team based" manufacturing is another type of bundling that combines some of the above characteristics. Developed in Japan, it is the grouping of sewing operators into teams of eight to ten. Rather than each sewer performing a single task, they work together on a garment from start to finish. One-third of the U.S. apparel industry has switched to either unit production or modular manufacturing. In Los Angeles, however, only a few major manufacturers engage in computerized unit productions (constituting about ten percent of total production) while the majority of contractors still use progressive bundling.

Because I specialized in plus size garments, my pattern pieces were large and Jim pointed out that I was wasting a lot of fabric. He asked if I had thought about doing anything else. That's when I came up with the idea of making kids' clothes. I made clothes for my grandchildren because I had huge pieces of left over fabric. When we established our factory, we learned to lay the pattern pieces on the marker to maximize fabric usage.

I taught my son to lay the pieces and he figured out if we laid the larger sizes combined with the smaller sizes, we got a better yield of fabric and saved money. The bundling method we chose to use is item bundling where all the pieces for a garment are tied in a group together.

> The AAMA Technical Advisory Committee (1993) reported that 80 percent of the apparel manufacturers used the bundle system of garment production. They also predicted that use of bundle systems for garment production would decrease as firms seek more flexibility in their production systems.

After everything is bundled you're ready to take the work out to the production floor. Before we get to that point, I learned to do a dry run to test production before we really got started. How do you do that? Well, we cut a dozen of the garments and assembled the components (elastic, trim, thread, etc.) and would sew one dozen pieces. That gave us a measure of the amount of time it would take us to produce a dozen and by doing this we could guesstimate the time that would be required for the entire run.

The dry run also helped us learn how to engineer the production. What were the things we needed to do first? Who was going to get the piece next? We had stations one through three, so if operator number one sewed the sides, someone else needed to have the elastic ready to go. By the time we got to station number three, we should have a finished product.

Quality Checklist

Quality checkpoints should be inserted at every station to ensure the garments are complete according to production specifications. Clearly, you don't want to finish a garment and find out the hem was sewn wrong or a seam is facing the wrong direction. That's the wrong time to find out the side is not correct. We learned to institute our quality control pieces at the critical points in production. The critical check points are at each work area and before joining the garment for completion.

After we performed our dry run, we were comfortable with how much time it was going to take, what stations were going to be set up, who was going to be at each station and what pieces were going to be sewn first, we were ready for production.

At the end of the production run, I instituted a final quality control check. We wanted to make sure all the strings were cut, there were no cracked buttons, the button holes were all sewn and the sleeves were the right length. There's nothing worse than getting a garment with one sleeve two inches longer than the other.

For your process, you want to check all pieces as you go through your quality control process. I developed a check sheet for the person conducting the final check, which would normally be my mom because she had a meticulous analytical method of spotting inconsistencies. As part of our operations process, we developed the criteria of a perfect garment coming out of production. To develop the best practices of quality control for our company, I analyzed and documented what a perfect garment should look like after it was completed. The documented items formed my quality control checklist. If a garment didn't meet the quality control criteria, it was pulled from the finished production bundle and it became an irregular to be sold during our sample sales or to an off-priced distributor. That being said, if you're dealing with hundreds of pieces, you need to have a dedicated resource to conduct the quality control, not sometimes, part-time or maybe here and there, but consistently checking the product using the developed process. The things you should look for when conducting your quality control check are:

- Open seams.
- Wrong stitching techniques
- Non-matching threads
- Hanging threads. You never should send a garment out with any thread hanging, they should all be clipped inside and out. You don't want to see thread hanging from the hem, cuffs or the collars.
- Missing stitches
- Broken or misaligned buttons. Buttons are supposed to be three inches apart and in a straight line.
- Improper creasing of the garment, like erroneous thread tension. If you're sewing fine silk, you don't want a super tight stitch that's going to crinkle the material.
- Raw edges. Everything should be sewn, so you never see raw edges.
- Color variations. Sometimes, even though you may order first quality or first goods, there may be a few imperfections. A lot of times when you unfold fabric, the first maybe couple of 10 yards are okay but when you get to the middle of the fabric, you've got problems with irregular weaving of the fabric.
- Fabric defects. That means pulled or loose yarn, holes in the fabric, rips or anything that is not a perfect piece of material.

- Short zippers
- Inappropriate trim
- Wrong size label in the garment

Stitching in the wrong size label is a serious mistake which deceives the store and the consumer. Here's a scenario. You walk into a trendy up-scale boutique and you spot the perfect little black dress. It is a size 2X and has your name all over it. Next step grab it and race for the dressing room. You unzip it, still thinking it looks a wee small, but you go for it only to be stopped because you can't get it over your hips nor can you comfortably slip your arm in the armhole. What a huge disappointment! You're upset, right!

Is it the stores fault? No, because they trust the manufacture to provide accurate sizes. A mislabeled garment causes the store owner to lose faith in you and your product. This situation bit us really, really hard. We did a run of size large, extra-large, 2X, 3X and 4X. Size large label was inadvertently stitched into the size 3X garments. Not good. Fortunately, by following our quality control process the error was caught, but label replacement is time consuming and ultimately cut my profit margin down because of the redundant work.

Just think if those garments were shipped incorrectly and how unhappy the woman who tried the dress on would be. So how and who is going to catch that problem in your operation?

Develop your quality control checklist – and USE it

Where is the best place to catch this kind of problem? A problem like this is caught when you bundle the cut pieces for the sewing operators to sew. Whoever is cutting the garment and bundling has to pay very close attention to all of the pieces that are going into that bundle. What do I mean here? Of course they are going to take care to watch the work, right? If you don't have a process in place, errors are multiplied many times over. The cutter should have a step-by-step procedure to follow to ensure the cut size is bundled with the correct size label. If not, when the cut pieces arrive at the sewing stations you have a huge mess on your hands.

Over time I've become competent at determining the size just by looking at a garment. You might say the wrong size label is an easy fix because it just entails pulling the label out and putting the right label in. If you have to perform that task for say 100 or 200 pieces, you're losing time. Time is money and you've got to ship it out the door so you won't have to eat the order. Eating the order means you won't be paid if you don't meet the shipping deadline. I'm happy to say I have never had to eat an order though we came close, but we do everything within our power to ship on time.

This quality control check sheet became our standard operating procedure that's on the wall for the entire operations staff to review.

To avoid shipping issues, embarrassment and non-payment, develop, implement and trust your quality control process. Your quality control process is your assurance to keep a good reputation among customers.

Chapter Seven

Packaging And Getting It Out Of the Door

Now that you've designed your garments, received your purchase order, produced the garments, and packaged them in garment bags, how do you ship it to the customer? To ensure the customer understands the options, I developed a document which outlines the carriers (UPS, FEDEX, and DHL) and shipping options such as ground, overnight, or 2Day, to discuss with the customer while writing the order. I ask the customer which method of shipment they would like to use.

To make life easy, the best method I've found is to open an account with each of the carriers. Prior to that I was haphazardly shipping via whoever I could call but it became more beneficial to have an account. Just call the company and say you would like to use their services and want to open an account. Of course, they'll give you the lengthy sales pitch and go through the steps, but the options available have become more small business friendly. Listed below is a screen shot of UPS' portal to open an account.

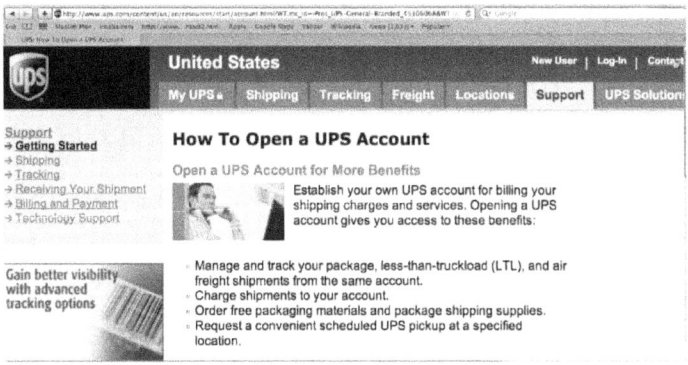

www.UPS.com

Packing Supplies

I found a wonderful packaging company in my city that supplied boxes, tape and envelopes at a great bulk rate. To eliminate wasted time, it is preferable to buy in bulk because the last thing you want to have happen is to run out of supplies and delay your shipment. I can talk about this with authority because it happened to me a few times. By not purchasing in bulk, it became an issue to get the shipping supplies in-house at the last minute and keeping them on hand.

When making your bulk purchase, all shipping components are critical, however, high on the list is shipping tape with little reinforcement strands in it because your boxes are going to be tossed all over the place and the last thing you want is to have your packages arrive at the store's facilities bursting at the seams or with lost components.

To determine the box size for product shipment, take the largest garment and fold it for shipping. Once folded, use this item as your guide to determine the width and length of the box needed to ship the garment with a substantial amount room between the box wall and the garment edge. If your test garment fits the box measurements, make this particular box your primary shipping component and build your shipping repertoire around the primary box.

Check with the supplier and tell them what you're shipping and they can give you some specifics on the type of box to use. The types of corrugated board for boxes are single face, single wall, double wall, and tri-wall corrugated board. I would suggest getting the strongest components because boxes can break in transit and you don't want to be held responsible for missing product. I keep an assortment of shipping supplies such as small, medium and large envelopes to ship small amounts, like one or two items. If you're shipping a half dozen or more of product, I would suggest using boxes.

For interior packaging, you can use what is called popcorn or bubble wrap. If you are environmentally conscious, my suggestion is to find an eco-friendly product. In the past rather than throw newspapers away, we crumpled it as filler in our boxes. I still use this practice to cut down as much as possible on paper waste.

Before a product is packed, you should perform one last quality control check. I developed a two-step quality control process for my facility. The first check is performed during the sewing process; while the second check is performed after the product is picked and ready for packing. During the check process your goal is to compare the components to be packed against a pick ticket.

Simply stated, a pick ticket is the delivery information; garment description, SKU (unique number/garment style number), and quantity to be shipped. As an audit trail, I have whoever picked the order sign off so that we know who to go back to if there is a problem. You should check the boxes before they go out the door to make sure that you have the right color and the right size according to the delivery information or pick ticket. I made a template of all these forms to keep in my standard operating procedure binder for future duplication.

Since we are a small business, typically the staff performs double duty, such as pick/pack and working in shipping and receiving. In the event there is a large order and the team needs help, those without a heavy workload pitch in to help with quality control and packing. After we finish production, the team assembles in the staging area at the back tables near the dock door and form groups to check product, pack and assemble it for the carrier to pick up.

Honestly, picking and packing is boring so to keep the spirits high we sing songs and make it a game. We make a line of boxes, get our pick tickets and go through each box to make sure the right components are included. Next step is to put a packing slip inside and seal the boxes. The packing slip is an itemized list which includes quantity description, style number unit of measure (each), of the product to be shipped. To complete the process, the team checks off each item and initial at the bottom of the form. Similarly, for your operation, set a criteria for the shipping crew for accountability. You want accountability in your operations as an audit trail to trace issues and make corrections.

After you're comfortable the order is correct, you've taped everything and called the carrier, you're ready to send the invoice. If you're conducting business with large retailers, you'll send the information electronically. If you're dealing with smaller vendors the customary approach is to take a 50% deposit at the time of writing the order. When it is time to ship the product, you or a designated person in your company will call the customer and tell them you are ready to ship.

Ask the customer which payment method they prefer to use credit card or PayPal. Process the payment and give them a shipment tracking number. If the card payment is successful, you get your payment and life is good. If the card fails, politely ask the customer for an alternate card and reprocess. If that card payment fails, again being very polite, inform the customer of the failure and give them other payment options. Put the order on hold until the customer pays for the shipment. **DO NOT SHIP**.

I've made the horrendous mistake of shipping then run the payment. This is a big O-M-G! In the past without a sound process in place, we were running around like crazy trying to get items in boxes and no one knew who was doing what, boxes were being shipped without payments, all kinds of goofy stuff going on simply because we lacked processes and organization.

Returns

So here's the scenario, the customer, for whatever reason, doesn't want the product. He or she calls you and says something like, "Hi, I'm calling because I just need to send this back, something is wrong, it doesn't look right". How do I send it back? I used to get these kinds of calls from small stores especially. The problem didn't have anything to do with product discrepancy. The customer usually had a change of heart after receiving the shipment. Maybe they really needed a smaller quantity than ordered or their cash flow was going in the negative direction, so returning the items, will give them the needed cash.

How do you handle returns? What do you do if the customer isn't happy after you ship? A RETURN POLICY!! Before the sale, be sure to document how you will process the inevitable product return. It's going to happen no matter how good your process or product is, you will receive returns as they are part of business operations. The key is how you/your business handle the customer service side of the return. The return itself will be fine. It is the customer you should be concerned about. Why? As much as possible you want to keep a good relationship with your beloved customer even under not-so-nice circumstances.

What should be the components of your return policy? Here's a partial list to help you develop your own.

- Time period in which returns are accepted
- Restocking fee
- Free or paid return shipping
- Call for return authorization
- If paying by credit card purchase price reversal when shipment is returned
- No damaged items accepted.
- Item in original package
- Tags attached

Let me share a quick story about returns. After a few months of cold calling to a customer, I was granted an appointment to give my presentation. Much to my relief, the customer bought several hundred dollars of merchandise. Boy was I happy, floating on cloud nine. Maybe twelve. So the order was processed, picked, packed, quality control conducted, and shipped. A few days later, I received a phone call from my customer who was terribly upset. He said the order was crap and he wasn't paying for damaged goods. The yelling and accusations of poor business practices were unsettling, but I put on my brave face and assured the customer he could return the product and receive a full refund.

Before ending our conversation, I asked what was wrong with the merchandise. He said that we sent defective product that was all ripped up. We were just floored and trying to figure out what happened because we wouldn't send out product like that. When we received the product, I asked the sewing contractor who sewed the garments to come to my office so we could review the garments.

I must tell you sewing operators, especially the women I work with, have a huge amount of pride in their work because they are artist and they love what they do and take great pride in producing high quality work. As we slowly opened the box to examine the dresses, much to our horror, each one of the dozen dresses had a six inch clean cut parallel to the side seam. Not in the seam but alongside the seam. Now, if someone stepped in the dress and split the dress because their hips were wide for the dress, the seam would have pulled apart. But this was a nice even clean cut, the type of cut made by a razor sharp knife.

We surmised this was the owner's way of getting out of paying us for the product. He didn't have courage enough to say he couldn't afford it or didn't want it. He said all the seams were ripped and the contractor said that it was a clean knife cut. Needless to say, we put him on the "DO NOT SELL TO THIS GUY" list. This was by far the most bizarre return case I encountered. Since I didn't have a return policy in place I refunded his money and called it a day. Lesson learned - institute a return policy to cover the bizarre return cases.

Summary:

- Develop a quality control process
- Develop a check list for pick and pack
- Develop audit sheet for packer to use
- Develop a product return policy

Chapter Eight

Doing Business With Large Retail Stores

It's all our hopes and dreams to get an order from let's say, Nordstrom, Neiman Marcus, Macy or one of the big retailers. Many designer's live for that day. For example, while exhibiting at a trade show you receive an order from a large retailer, what's the next step? There are a myriad of steps to fill the order from a big retailer. Among the myriad of steps, suppliers are expected to be EDI compliant. EDI compliant is the ability to conduct business, receiving purchase orders, sending ship notices and invoices electronically. Conducting business electronically with large retailers means you're now entering the world of electronic data interchange or EDI.

Electronic Data Interchange (EDI)

EDI was developed in the United States in the mid 1960's by the railroads. It was a way for them to communicate information via a standard format, and that standard format is called X12. There's a standard suite of documents that are traded in the X12 format between companies. They are purchase order (850), purchase order confirmation (855), Purchase order change (860), advance shipping notice (856), and invoice (810). If you need a list of the EDI transactions, you can use the Internet to conduct a search for EDI transactions in order to gain familiarity with the terminology

When you receive a purchase order from a large retailer, they will ask if you are you EDI capable. What they are asking is do you have the capability to send or receive information electronically via the X12 format. Quick story - While exhibiting at a tradeshow in Las Vegas, NV I was approached by a large distribution company who was very interested in my product. During my follow-up call with the representative, I asked if the company was EDI capable. Long pause. The young lady finally took a breath and said, "Oh yeah, you can send me an email with your order. We do that." Shall I say it was an interesting conversation!

If you're a newbie and you receive a big order, you're going to have to scramble rather quickly because it is expensive to implement EDI. However, there are services that will help you set up the process. Many of them are on the Internet, but you should also ask the vendor if they have a web solution to transmit documents.

A web solution, an order entry website, is an on-line portal for suppliers. For example, if you are not setup with EDI and the vendor has a supplier website/portal, your company will be given an id and password to login to the dedicated site and enter your order.

The other alternative is to work with an EDI outsource company to get you setup to send orders and receive payment from the large retailer.

What the EDI service will provide:

1. Develop data maps for the electronic documents
2. Send your documents to your trading partner
3. Handle Errors
4. Setup new customers for you

The most prominent benefit for using EDI with your trading partner (the store) is speed and accuracy of receiving and fulfilling orders. For example, where it would take days via snail mail, sending the order via EDI reduces the time from days to minutes. Moreover, there is a reduction in typographical errors. In the view of the vendor, using EDI will make the vendor/supplier order process more efficient and reduce time spent correcting information, customer phone calls, and increased business from the customer.

Advanced Shipping Notice (ASN)

The Advanced Shipping Notice or ASN is a critical document in the industry because it conveys to the store what orders are on the truck and the delivery date. Other pertinent pieces of data are the product detail, quantities shipped and label information. Below is a list of data sent on an ASN:

1. Bill of Lading (BOL)
2. Shipment Number
3. Carrier information - Trucking company name
4. Number of deliveries on the truck
5. Purchase orders associated with the deliveries
6. Container number - Number used on a box or carton to uniquely identify it

The ASN is a time sensitive document and must reach the distribution center before the truck carrying the actual order. In the event the truck reaches its destination prior to the ASN, the cargo will sit on the dock unopened waiting for the shipping notice to arrive. Undocumented shipments wreak havoc at a store's distribution center because it holds up other customer orders which need to be processed into the center and delays shipment to the destination store. If the ASN doesn't arrive, the warehouse staff will have to manually process the shipment.   Prior to the manual process procedure, the vendor's EDI department will send nasty grams and make ugly phone calls demanding an explanation as to why you have not sent the ASN and when it will be sent.

With the larger retailers, if you don't ship on time, and don't send the ASN within the ship window, you will be fined for non-compliance with the company's shipping guidelines. Now you're entering the world of the dreaded chargeback. If you didn't complete all the information on your ASN, something is missing, you'll get a friendly email that says your ASN has been rejected and by the way the charge is $100 per carton on the truck because you didn't provide the right information. Some of them, depending on the store, will charge you $100 per each incorrect ASN.

What does that do to your bottom line? Let's say your order is $10,000 and you have 40 cartons in the shipment and the chargeback amount is $100.00 per carton. Multiply 40 cartons times $100.00 which is $4,000.00. See the example for the calculations.

Purchase Order Amount	$10,000.00
Chargeback Amount	- $4,000.00
Balance Due To You	$6,000.00

The above example is a fairly small order and the chargeback amount is small as well. However, as you grow your business and trade more purchase orders at higher dollar amounts, noncompliance becomes very costly.

To avoid the costly chargebacks, it is very important that you and your warehouse personnel pay strict attention to routing and compliance guidelines and make sure you deliver the product within the customer's ship window or else you will be charged.

Entering the world of the big retailers and shipping to one of the biggest stores in the country can be a nightmare, and it can ruin you financially rather quickly. Another component of the business process which can deplete your finances is lack of funds for order fulfillment and the wait time to receive your payment. Depending on the payment terms you negotiate, the wait time can be as long as 45 to 60 days.

NOTE**** Securing the help of a factor early on in the process can help financially while you wait to get paid from your vendor.

If you do incur a charge back/non-compliance fee, you could likely face the situation of owing the vendor. It's important to understand that as a small vendor thirsting after that big dream order and entering the electronic arena; there are some pitfalls and big dog bites that will come after you. If you can't handle it yourself, save yourself frustration and outsource your EDI operation to a reputable EDI service who can help you set up the data mapping and walk you through the process.

Routing

When I talk about routing, it means the instructions the vendor gives you about how to ship to them - in other words which carrier and methods they prefer to use for shipments. To view the routing information go to the stores website and drill down to the EDI section to find the routing tab. On this site the store lists which carrier they want to use and how they want you to ship.

Typically the supplier pays for shipping so you must calculate this cost into the price of your garments.   The vendor will tell you how to pack and ship the product. They will want all sizes or specific sizes packed in separate cartons. There may be a stipulation that you can't mix the sizes or mix the colors in one carton. In addition, there may be a breakdown on the store's EDI site explaining a designated carrier will be used for certain shipment weights.

For example, let's say one of the large retailers places an order for one of your most popular dresses with a total weight under 80,000 pounds. In this example, the store prefers the supplier to use carrier ABCD. If the weight is over 80,000 pounds, then use carrier EFGH.

For small parcels, usually individual items, UPS or FEDEX is the preferred carrier. Orders of this nature are normally orders to individuals from your e-commerce site. The type of shipment handling will be indicated as ground, 2 day, 3 day or over-night.

The vendor will also stipulate how the labels should be printed. When you're dealing with the large department stores, they have what is known in the industry as Mark-For, which means the order is destined for a particular store but is shipped to the associated distribution center (DC). When the order arrives at the DC, it will be sent to the specific store or it is stored on-site for a future ship date. That's why it's incredibly important that the shipping label be accurate. The warehouse personnel don't want the hassle of determining the destination store.

Mark-For Store/Distribution Center

As discussed earlier, product is marked for a store but sent to a DC or Distribution Center. The information is communicated via UCC 128 label, which has been renamed DS1 labels.

Label information is documented in the supplier's guideline usually within the vendors EDI website. Components on the label are the purchase order number, the department, the company name, the company address, the store number, and the product description. If any one of these pieces of information is missing you'll be charged. The products may be packed in the right box but the information on the label is incorrect and is considered a compliance infraction.

In the order-to-cash process, the DC is the central point for order receipt by large retailers. Typically, orders come to you from a department store and they will send you the Mark-For store in the incoming data but do not send the associated DC, so you're playing a guessing game. Which DC do you use? If it's not in the data, your outsource EDI department should know the correlation between the DC and the store. When the EDI department receives the store number, they should have a lookup table that confirms which DC the store is associated with. During the planning phase you and your EDI staff or the outsource EDI department develop a fact finding process to obtain all the stores and associated DCs from the vendor to setup the data mapping correctly, because if you don't understand it, too many times small vendors have literally have gone out of business due to lack of knowledge.

The thing to remember with EDI is to work with the routing guys, make sure your labels are correct and that you're in compliance. Sometimes the vendor may send an email indicating a change in the DC store relationship. For example, 10 stores which will now ship out of DC "XYZ" rather than DC "FGH". It's your responsibility to stay abreast of the compliance and routing information or to work with your outsource department to understand that you're in compliance or else you risk substantial fines.

Universal Product Codes (UPC)

Universal Product Code, is a unique 12-digit number assigned to retail merchandise that identifies both the product and the vendor that sells the product. The UPC on a product typically appears adjacent to its bar code, the machine-readable representation of the UPC.

The first six digits of the UPC are the vendor's unique identification number. All of the products that one vendor sells will have the same first six digits in their UPCs. The next five digits are the products unique reference number that identifies the product within any one vendor's line of products. The last number is called the check digit that is used to verify that the UPC for that specific product is correct.

Within your business process, you should have assigned style numbers to your garments by category. In addition, each item will also be assigned a UPC. For instance, if you're selling sleeveless A-line dresses, whatever that style number is, you will have a UPC number that is associated with it. Let me give a specific example.

I have a princess line long sleeve, ankle length dress - style 3001 in my database. Internally, my staff knows the description of style 3001. However, my trading partner doesn't know style 3001 and really doesn't care. When my customer places a purchase order with me they will order by the UPC <u>NOT</u> the style number. Therefore in my database I assign style 3001 to UPC 430071639853. So my database would have entries like:

Ann-Nayarit Style # Category Dresses	UPC
3001	430071639853
3002	430071639854
3003	430071639855
3004	430071639856
3005	430071639857

Because large retailers only order by UPC numbers, I strongly suggest start assigning all your sku numbers to a UPC number and communicating that information back to the store. They do not deal with style number, will not send a style number, and will always send a UPC number. There are companies on the Internet where you can buy UPC numbers. However, please note, if you purchase a small block of UPC numbers from the company, the identifying numbers belong to their company and not to you. I suggest finding companies which will allow you to purchase blocks of UPC numbers associated solely with your company. Go to GS1.com or you can search for them on the Internet to purchase UPC number blocks.

EAN Codes

If the event you should receive a large order from a European retailer, keep in mind they use what's called the EAN. It's just like a UPC but it has extra digit. As with the purchase of UPC(s) your best option is to buy an entire block which represents your company.

EDI is a key component to your company's future growth. The best way to grow is to become knowledgeable about EDI and how it will benefit your relationship if you conduct business with a large retailer. If you intend to work with a large retailer take the time now to lay the foundation in your business to implement an EDI solution rather than wait for the first order to come in.

Summary - Benefits of EDI

1. Faster processing
2. Reduced fees for doing business electronically
3. Reduced purchase order errors
4. Faster payment

Chapter Nine

Creating Buzz and Stealth Marketing

Earlier we talked about knowing your market, how you get to know them and what you need to do. Once you find out who they are, how do you get in their face? Is it through advertising? No, it's not through advertising alone, the method is called marketing. In the early days of my business, I didn't have a lot of bucks and I thought publicity and marketing and advertising were the same thing, but I was wrong. Many new people in business make the same assumption.

To get your name out there, you have to get publicity. Publicity is the notice or attention given to someone or something by the media. So when you do things like sponsor a cookout for a little league baseball team, sponsor a health fair, or walk-a-thon, you want to spread the word. So how do you let people know what you're doing? You let the world know through press releases sent to the media.

That begs the question, how do you do this with no money or at low cost? It's easy as pie, I say that now after losing thousands of dollars in advertising that didn't give the desired results. I want

to help you save money and get your name out there. Here are some things you can do that I consider low cost or no cost.

Press Release

You can write a press release which is easy and free. It takes a little time, but this is how you tell local newspapers or radio stations about your business activity.

For every activity your company participates in, send out a press release to the media. I keep a template so when I'm ready to write a press release, I just fill in my template and I don't have to recreate the wheel. I must confess, I may sound like an authority now but in my startup days, I often recreated the wheel and was spinning my wheel kicking up a lot of sand. Believe me, I stressed more than anything over writing these press releases because I didn't understand how to strategically write them or use them. Once I mastered that skill set, I could confidently write a press release to my target audience. The press release isn't the only way to expose your business to clients. You can use Facebook, Twitter and YouTube.

YOUTUBE

Let's talk about free and making an impact. YouTube has exploded and become a must have tool in the entrepreneur's marketing arsenal. To film a video you don't need fancy expensive equipment. An inexpensive camcorder will suffice. So what will you film? Film yourself talking about a subject matter that's of interest to the client, then pop it up on YouTube and put a link on your website and provide video on a consistent basis to do two things. One to build you search engine optimization and build your credibility as an authority on your subject matter. The YouTube videos make you an authority, because you're seen as a person that's adding value.

It's easy to load and send a link, whether it is emailed or embedded on your social media page, I love to tell people to go check out my video. I did a video on how to coordinate colors and styles. What I did is to recruit models to come in, have them model my clothes while I talked about the benefits my clothes provide to the customer. We did a 20 minute segment using my clothes, paneled skirts, and how to pair for them for the summer, which colors to pick and which shoes to wear. I became a mini authority on high-end modest-wear and received hits from this.

Not to mention it boost my rank on the search engines.

You can also write letters to the editor of your local paper. Be professional and kind, but write something that's interesting and/or noteworthy. Pay attention to the current headlines and comment on them to the editor. You'll be surprised how often your letter will be printed and you'll build credibility with the media.

Other things you can do is blog on your website. Tell your story and provide tips, give people something that's helpful, something that will solve a problem. Blogging is also a method for building credibility as an authority in your industry. Talk about a current affair, give tips, and chronicle your journey or anything else that's current.

Another free method to showcase your business is to attend and network at events. You may be shy like me, but there's a way to work those networking events.

Initially, I just couldn't bring myself to talk about my business because I viewed it as boasting or bragging which my mom told me never to do. So you see I had a barrier to overcome. To overcome the emotional hurdle, I thought of myself as a subject matter expert (SME) and practiced giving tips about a fashion business startup based on my mistakes. To help me remember what to say, I developed bullet points or talking points. Be sure to always carry and handout out business cards strategically. I say strategically because there may be particular people you want to meet and engage. Before attending an event, I call the sponsor and ask who is the target market of the networking event. If it is a market I want to reach the next question is who are the professionals attending the function. For example, if I am attending a wedding planners networking event, I'll ask if photographers, videographers and boutique owners are attending. If yes then I build my plan of attack. At the event target the people you want to meet and, most important, get a business card from them and start a database so you can periodically send out information about what you're doing and explore ways you can collaborate.

Another easy and free thing you can do, which I like to do, is public speaking. I go to the library and rent one of the conference rooms for a nominal fee. I pick a date, put out flyers and my talk is free. In my talk, I tell the audience about my business, but I talk to the audience about self-help techniques they can readily employ to move their business forward, and how my company can be of benefit to them. The purpose of the speech is what I call a "give back speech", but at the back of the room I provide my company's brochures for lead generation and follow-up. On my brochure is my website, email address and phone number. But most importantly, I have a customer sign-in form so I can collect the attendee's names for future contact.

Most libraries won't allow you to sell products; however, if people want further services from you, ask them to sign your list and go to your website and sign up for further services. When you hold these public speaking events, have your assistant ask them to fill out a survey that includes pertinent information such as their name, address and email address. If they want to give you a phone number, that's great but the email address is a must.

Take that information and actively engage them because they've signed up and given you permission to market directly to them. If they ask how to get in touch with you, always make sure you have a nice card with your contact information, email address, website and phone number.

You can also carry other people's business cards with you because you want to be seen as a valuable resource. If someone asks you for a service you don't provide, you can tell them that you are not the person to service them but you happen to have the contact information of someone who can service them.

To stay at the top of my customer's mind, I like to send out promotions with invoices. When I send out packages I include discount coupons for the customer's next order and other promotional material. What this activity does is build your name/brand in their psyche and you become a trusted resource - the go-to person when they are ready to buy.

To stay top of my customer's mind I engage them using email marketing. My favorites are Constant Contact and iContact, but there are host of other similar services for you to choose from. There are other websites I've used in order to get publicity information when I need to get ideas such as Mad Mimi. To investigate other email products, use the internet to search for them by using the search term "email marketing".

There are many websites that publish valuable material about publicity and how to get it. One such site is Bill Stoehler's publicity website. Bill Stoehler puts out a really great newsletter, and I've received a lot of helpful tips from him. Another great source is

Joan Stewart's Publicity Hound website and newsletter, who over the years, has given multiple tips on how to pitch to the media. Though pitching is critical, unfortunately I didn't understand these steps up front. Over time I've learned to utilize press releases, pitch to the media and use email marketing efficiently. I had no problem calling TV show producers, but I wasn't saying the right things to get their attention.

So, if you're pitching to the media, take time to do the research, learn how to present a subject matter to them that will allow them to think of you as a resource to put on TV or radio. After learning how to pitch to the media, I've been on radio many times in my local area. I've gone on afternoon shows to talk about the business or being a woman entrepreneur.

Stay engaged in the community and always let them know what you're doing. You can sponsor community events that won't break your wallet or partner with another company and produce a community event. One thing I did was to donate product to a local hospital's breast cancer center. You can find places to donate and then write about it in a press release and send it to the media. Even if it's not printed, if it goes out online and someone searches for you, your name will come up and more often than not they'll see how much you do and are engaged, which leads them to view you as an authority and an expert in your field.

Reporter Websites

A website I highly recommend is The Reporter Connection, which you can sign up for at www.ReporterConnection.com. This newsletter provides a variety of resources as well as places where you can write and submit your own articles about what you do, tips you're providing and other information for people.

Summary

Keeping your name in front of your audience is critical to your business survival - remember the saying, "Out of sight out of mind". You want to be top of mind when the customer needs your services. Here are a few summary tips:

- Use press releases
- Use Videos
- Use direct email
- Use community sponsorships

Chapter Ten

Invest In Yourself

"Seek knowledge from the cradle to the grave"
-- Prophet Muhammad(pbup)

As busy entrepreneurs, our days and nights are consumed with building our brand and moving our businesses to the next level. But you can't manage your business if your physical and emotional health are failing. In order for your business to grow and flourish you have to rest your body, calm your mind and consistently learn new things. What shall I learn? How do I carve time out of my schedule for the learning activity? You know, it is easier than it appears. With a myriad of on-line courses such as marketing, business and writing, carving out time is a matter of discipline.

The best approach is to get involved in a learning activity that isn't mentally taxing. Moreover, the activity should be relaxing but thought provoking. If writing is your weakness, then enroll in a creative writing class. Although creative writing may appear to be unrelated to fashion design, the nuances of creative writing will bolster your writing confidence and thus have an immediate impact on your writing ability to produce press releases or other copy for your company. Maybe painting strikes your fancy so you enroll in a painting class at your local junior college. Beyond relaxation, participating in a group activity offers the chance to meet potential customers or persons with whom you can form partnerships. As entrepreneurs we wear multiple hats, run at a very fast pace and oftentimes overburden ourselves with more work than we should. To decrease the chances of burn-out or serious health challenges, it's important to take time to physically relax our brain as well as our bodies.

Relaxing our bodies can be accomplished through several techniques such as routine walking, aerobic exercise or yoga. Pick an exercise routine that works for you. Yoga is my favorite way of relaxing. If there's an exercise facility near you, such as a fitness center, check out the classes offered and find a time that you can make a part of your schedule. If you are not able to get in a gym workout, take time in the early morning, even if you have to get up a little earlier, to get outside to exercise or walk. I find that taking long walks help to clear my mind of clutter and internal noise. If I'm really stressed, I'll walk a bit extra than my usual walking pattern. This gives me an opportunity to think of new ideas because in the fashion industry the customer is always looking for the latest, greatest and the newest. In order to think creatively, I have to be in a relaxed frame of mind. You may have to experiment with relaxation methods that are most beneficial for you.

If you don't keep a journal, consider starting one and jot down daily notes to yourself whether business or personal. Take time to write to yourself or your loved ones or perhaps submit your pieces to a literary magazine or your local newspaper for publication.

Writing is certainly a method that can be relaxing as well as improve your overall skill set. Something else you can do to increase your skill set is to attend industry seminars. They can be incredibly helpful because you'll talk to people in the industry that will give you fuel for new concepts. For example, there is a new concept for fitting called 3D fitting. I wouldn't have known about it if I hadn't been looking at an industry journal and attended an industry function. If you're going to compete in the industry, it's important to keep abreast of current trends by reading trade journals and attending seminars.

On a more personal note, when I say to invest in yourself, perhaps the idea of financial investment in the business venture is top of the mind, but what about investing in a new wardrobe to create a new you; this is an emotional boost versus a learning activity. The feel good routine is what I call it; something that makes you feel good about yourself. As entrepreneurs, we can become mentally fatigued. The mental fatigue can cause grumpiness, lack of will power to make well informed decisions or irritability. It's a simple matter to upgrade your image. For women, it can be something as simple as a new skirt or a nice crisp blouse or scarf, something simple can give you the confidence to stand in front of a client and give a presentation about your collection. For men it can be anything from a new pair of shades to a new designer shirt which hopefully you'll wear proudly.

Develop New Industry Skills

As we're looking at new wardrobes and updating our personal self, we have to also develop our fashion skill sets. To decide what to improve, take a sheet of paper and divide it into two columns. In one column write down your current skills, in the second column write down skills you would like to improve or new skills you would like to learn. You may need to improve your communication skills by enrolling in a continuing education class in public speaking. An alternative to the continuing education route is to join Toastmasters because, the cost is minimal and you'll meet fabulous people.

To successfully compete in the fashion industry, one must continue to improve acquired skills. Maybe you already know how to sketch and make a pattern so you think you're well versed in the fashion industry, but don't rest on your laurels. To stay fresh and ahead of the curve, enroll in industry seminars, workshops, or on-line classes. You can take classes in advanced draping or pattern making, maybe learn something about pattern making that you don't know.

Another significant thing you can do is hire a coach. Even though we may know a lot, in order to move to the next level, we may need to have someone hold us accountable and push us out of our comfort zone. Hiring a coach or mentor can assist you, whether it's a speaking coach, writing coach or health trainer, it's important to have a coach. A coach or mentor is someone who will hold you accountable for your actions and push you to do better in whatever it is you're striving for in your long and short-term goals. If you don't hire a coach, you'll have your to-do list and set goals, but life gets in the way and sometimes we get in our own way. To help us get out of our way, that's where a coach or mentor comes in. In some cases a coach/mentor can be a person you admire but have not personally met. That's OK. Study their mannerism and emulate their ideas and strategies.

Whatever you choose, exercise, painting, writing poetry, sailing or cycling find time to rejuvenate and grow. You have a tremendous job ahead of you to make a purposeful impact on the world by leaving your footprint on humanity. Do it! Take the step, the first step toward your new life. Whether you choose to enter the fashion world as a manufacturer, stylist, make-up artist, hair stylist or fashion blogger, take the step. Make the move. Be enthusiastic and help someone along the way to start their journey.

The first step maybe wobbly and painfully scary but take it. Standup and place your foot squarely in front of you with the intention in your heart to move forward never looking back but with your head held high with a true sense of purpose. Chart your course through your business and marketing plan. Place pictures around your office, bedroom, kitchen and living room of the life you want to lead.

The road may become narrow, laden with rocks and thorny vines, but hold fast to your goal and God's hand. Be mindful of how you treat others while pursuing your goal, for your actions good or bad will certainly come back to you --- multiplied.

This is not the end of the book. No, this is an adventure that is only getting better. I'm grateful that I have been able to help others and I feel obligated to do so because there have been many many people along the way who have helped me immensely and I'm eternally grateful to God for sharing these beautiful people with me.

Keep Moving Forward,
Sumiyyah

www.ingramcontent.com/pod-product-compliance
Lightning Source LLC
Chambersburg PA
CBHW051654170526
45167CB00001B/465